D0976483

BROKEN BUT LOVED

BROKEN BUT LOVED

Healing through Christ's Power

by

George A. Maloney, S.J.

ALBA · HOUSE   NEW · YORK

SOCIETY OF ST. PAUL, 2187 VICTORY BLVD., STATEN ISLAND. NEW YORK 10314

Library of Congress Cataloging in Publication Data

Maloney, George A., 1924-
    Broken but loved.

    Includes bibliographical references.
    1. Jesus Christ—Person and offices. 2. Christian
life—Catholic authors. I. Title. II. Title:
Healing through Christ's power.
BT202.M316   232   81-1802
ISBN 0-8189-0411-9   AACR2

Imprimi Potest:
Vincent M. Cooke, S.J.
Provincial of New York Province
September 2, 1980

Designed, printed and bound in the United States of
America by the Fathers and Brothers of the
Society of St. Paul, 2187 Victory Boulevard,
Staten Island, New York 10314, as part of their
communications apostolate.

---

    4 5 6 7 8 9 (Current Printing: first digit).

ACKNOWLEDGEMENTS

Sincere thanks to Mrs. Rita Ruggiero for typing this manuscript; to Andrea Federoff for her suggestions and corrections that proved most helpful. A special thanks to the anonymous writer of the poem, *Reverse Creation* that I have inserted into the other poems that I wrote for this book by way of meditations. Grateful acknowledgement is made to the following publishers: Darton, Longman & Todd, Ltd., and Doubleday & Company, Inc. All scriptural texts are from this Bible version unless otherwise noted.

DEDICATION

To Clarence Dionne, a man gifted by God with a power to love all whom he meets and heal them of their fears and loneliness.

CONTENTS

CONTENTS

INTRODUCTION

O ne of the realities that constantly face all of us is our brokenness.
When we, as Christians, hear the word, *brokenness*, we might
think of how God has dealt with us to "break us" of our proud
complacency. I have used this word throughout this book to describe
the "not yet" condition in which we find ourselves from the first
moment of birth until the last moment before our final death. It refers
to all the elements in our lives that prevent Jesus from being totally our
Lord and Master.

Such a condition is shared to some degree in common by all of us.
The Church wisely recognizes this in its constant teaching of the
doctrine of original sin. There is sin in our members, as St. Paul
confesses (Rm 7:23), that prevents us in our brokenness from being
whole, integrated, healed and holy children of God.

Moreover, our daily experiences show us that we also add to our
own personal brokenness. We find it much easier to be self-centered
than to be patient and loving to all whom we meet. We would like to be
holy, like the great saints of old, but we so often fall into mediocre
tepidity.

Some Christians build up an ideal person and ignore their existential brokenness as they imagine that they can become that ideal person
without coming to grips with their brokenness. Others are very much
aware of their inability to be loving since they find those lamentable
areas deeply within their inner selves exerting much negative influence to make them even more broken. Such persons readily accept
their broken condition and settle down to a cold war existence with
their inner "enemy."

JESUS HEALS

I n this book I develop the theme of brokenness but my purpose is to show that our healing comes from Jesus Christ. No matter how broken and dark our condition is, we can be healed and brought into the light of Jesus Christ. This book is rooted in Christian realism. It seeks to stir the reader to meditate upon each topic of brokenness presented by a poetic meditation concluding each chapter. Not only must we acknowledge the full extent of our collective and personal brokenness, but we must believe in the healing power of Jesus to effect a new creation, as St. Paul assures us (2 C 5:17-19).

DARKNESS IN GOD

I n order that our sinful condition be not too ominous, I begin this book focused on God in His infinite love for us. God is love (1 Jn 4:8). He is unceasingly pouring out His love for each of us. Such a loving movement of God in self-giving toward us has been usually described in Holy Scripture as the light and glory of God. He is perfect and immutable in his love and holiness. "God is light; there is no darkness in him at all" (1 Jn 1:5).

But God in Jesus Christ loves us so much that He enters into our human brokenness He not only gives us His love, but God displays His true beauty and holiness in waiting in awful, suffering expectancy that Holy Scripture likens to a presence of God in the cloud of darkness.

BROKENNESS IN JESUS

J esus comes as the Suffering Servant to reveal that God's weakness in waiting for our response is His true, healing, loving power. Jesus consents to expose Himself to the evil and brokenness of our human condition. All of His earthly life He moves from darkness to light, from temptation to sin, tempted as we (Heb 4:15) to perfect obedience to the Father's will.

In the desert Jesus was tempted, as a model of His entire earthly existence, to remain in our human brokenness by refusing to stretch out in the healing love of the Father. "For our sake God made the sinless one into sin" (2 C 5:21). He struggled as we to let God become His Father at every moment. Not by bread alone, nor presumptive power or worldly possessions would Jesus become the human expression of the Heavenly Father's love for us, but only by a gentle spirit of loving obedience.

A BROKEN SOCIETY

O nce we have seen that God in Jesus Christ and His Spirit of love is close to us in our brokenness, we can afford to look at the human scene. There we encounter a broken world, a society of monads that have forgotten how to speak the universal language of love that heals by union. We have the courage to accept the collective guilt of a nation that has for long believed that God thinks as we think and hates as we hate.

Even in our Churches we are confronted with cultic sinfulness, schisms and heresies that have rent the Body of Christ into fragmented parts. We face a Church, called to be the Bride of Christ and the Mother of our children of God, but so often in history appearing as the adulterous wife of Hosea in need of conversion and reform.

I AM BROKEN

B ut then we need to zero in upon our own personal history of brokenness. From time to time in prayer we do unveil somewhat the masks and posturing before God, others and even ourselves to discover what an abyss of darkness and sin lies within us. We pray King David's Psalm 51 with greater realism and conviction:

> Have mercy on me, O God, in your goodness,
> in your great tenderness wipe away my faults;
> wash me clean of my guilt,
> purify me from my sin (Ps 51:1-2).

What fears plague and cripple us! How unfree we are to love as children of God ought!

A HEALING SAVIOR

I s there some way out of the depths of darkness? Are we predestined to live in such brokenness all the days of our lives? Christianity gives us the saving hope in Jesus the Savior. He is the Way to full healing. He comes to bring us life that we might have it more abundantly (Jn 10:10). As He walked on this earth and touched the broken ones, broken in body, soul or spirit, and He healed them as they believed in Him, so the Church teaches that we can still be touched by Him through the sacraments and the preached Word and receive from Him a share in His eternal life.

We can be healed of the scars of the past. Future brokenness can be avoided by our accepting the present moment as a gift and a call to new life. Jesus becomes healer of our brokenness in any shape or form if we call out to Him with expectant hope and loving surrender to let Him be completely Lord in our lives. "Lord, Jesus Christ, Son of God, have mercy on me a sinner!"

A BROKEN HEALER

To the degree that we are healed by God's love incarnated in Jesus, to that degree God will use us to be His healing hands of love to others, more broken than we are. God's humility is shown in His need for human beings to manifest His active love for the world. He needed Abraham, Moses, the Prophets. He needed a woman so that His Son could become in human form His eternal love for us. Jesus needed or consented to need twelve Disciples upon whom He built His Church.

And Jesus still needs us, broken limbs of the Vine, but now healed by His Spirit of love, to become channels of His healing love for others. We can become healers of the world's brokenness primarily by intercessory prayer, as we offer the propitiation of Jesus Christ, the High-Priest, to the Father. Love begets love and brings about the healing that God calls all of us to bring, firstly, to those whom He has gifted us in our families. Such healing is slow, but unfolds in the stable monotony of family and community commitment.

Jesus is the answer to the world's estrangement and broken disharmony. But it is the whole Jesus, the total Body of Christ, with His members that brings His healing love into the world. This book is written not only for the broken people of the world, but, above all, it is a call to such to become healed by His power and go forth in the same power of His loving Spirit to bring healing and wholeness to a world that knows so much brokenness.

George A. Maloney, S.J.

CHAPTER ONE

DARKNESS IN GOD

F or most of us night is an ambivalent experience. As children, we feared to walk through a cemetery at night. When we were fever-ridden on a sickbed, we longed for the heavy shadows of night to release their hold on us and yield to the brightness of day. The night is dark and ominous. It fills us with fears and anxieties. Shadows play on our imagination as we mistake what seemingly appears to be for what we think it really is.

Yet night is also for us a time of peace and rest. After much fatiguing work, rapid movement, clamoring noises, the sun sets and we with all of nature enter into a slower rhythm of life. Peace and oneness between ourselves and all of nature take over in the growing darkness. We take our rest in sleep that restores our strength.

But night also unites us in our homes with our loved ones. It is a call to intimacy and love. It is a movement from doing to being as we love and are loved into new levels of caring and being cared for. It is a time to meet God in deep prayer. We learn to rest in His presence. Darkness of night seems to allow us to darken the light of our rational control over God and to enter into a new way of "seeing" in the night of faith.

At night in prayer we enter into the primal symbol not only of the darkness in us but of that which is in God. As we return to God as the Beginning and the End of our existence, we learn to worship Him and surrender ourselves to Him more completely, more totally. "Stretch out your hands toward the sanctuary, bless Yahweh night after night!" (Ps 134:2).

LIGHT AND DARKNESS

B ut even to infer that in God there could be any darkness amounts to
a blasphemy. For does not our whole Christian tradition present
God as light? "God is light; there is no darkness in him at all" (Jn 1:5).
"The Word was the true light that enlightens all men" (Jn 1:9). God
dwells in eternal light and Jesus brings that light into our world (Jn
8:12).

Light becomes more than a physical life when applied to God.
Being light, He is the fullness of reality, of perfection. There can be no
imperfection or darkness in Him. This makes God eternally the same,
all perfect, immutable. Change in God would denote a darkness or
imperfection in Him.

And so we associate darkness with evil, the kingdom of Satan,
Hell, the underworld. Sin and death are personified in terms of
darkness and ugliness.[1] Darkness is dirt, filth, unreality.

Yet, when we look more closely into Holy Scripture, we find that
God is often associated with darkness. Although seen in Himself, God
is perfect and without change, pre-existing Source of all being and
utterly independent of any other person. But when God is presented,
especially in the Old Testament, as Yahweh, the *One-toward-us*, He
is seen as present and communicating Himself to His chosen people in
darkness, shadow and a cloud.

Often God communicates with His prophets in visions and in
dreams.

> If any man among you is a prophet
> I make myself known to him in a vision,
> I speak to him in a dream (Nb 12:6).

It was in the dead of night that Yahweh delivered the Israelites
from the Egyptians (Ex 11:8-13). That night was unto destruction for
many of the Egyptians, but for God's chosen people it was the
passover, the night of redeeming deliverance.

God dwells in darkness in reference to His created world. "Darkness he made a veil to surround him" (Ps 18:11). "Cloud and
Darkness surround him, Righteousness and Justice support his
throne" (Ps 97:2). Yahweh guided His desert people in the form of a
pillar of cloud by day (Ex 13:21). And when Moses was invited to

meet God on top of Mount Sinai, it was from within the darkness of the cloud that God spoke to him (Ex 24:16-17).

GOD TOWARD US

There is no contradiction between light and darkness in God. Whenever Holy Scripture associates light with God, such texts refer either to God's self-contained, perfected Being, as independent of any relationship to His created order, or to God's final, eschatological glory which He shares with a fulfilled cosmos that has become "reconciled" to Him at the end of time.

Darkness is the archetypal symbol that is used in Scripture to refer to God as He *humbly* condescends to become present in His communicating love to us human beings. "Shadow," for example in Scripture, is an image to express the special protection of God over His people.[2] Reference to darkness surrounding God is a biblical way of expressing God's stretching out in affectivity, in caring, to be lovingly concerned and self-involved in giving Himself to mankind.

The late Abraham Heschel, one of America's leading Jewish theologians, in his work, *The Prophets*, uses the word *pathos* to describe God's "being in a personal and intimate relation to the world . . . a living care, a dynamic relation between God and the world . . . (God's) constant concern and involvement . . . an emotional engagement."[3]

From the Old Testament and also the experience that Jesus had of His heavenly Father, as recorded in the New Testament, God is a pursuing Lover. He is open and giving of Himself in faithful, committed love that is proved by His involved actions towards His beloved children. He is, therefore, vulnerable, humble, waiting, ready to suffer the insolence and indifference of human beings.[4]

AN EARTHY GOD

The biblical God is an earthy God. He loves His created world and sees that it is "very good" (Gn 1:18). But His love, as Jesus reveals to us, is God's very own presence within matter whereby He gives Himself to us human beings by His immanent actions. Jesus defends Himself before the Scribes and Pharisees for having worked a healing on the Sabbath by pointing out that His Father is always actively working out of love for all of His creatures. "My father goes on working, and so do I" (Jn 5:19).

God is a giving God in His loving activities. But precisely because the biblical concept of God places Him so immediately present and immanently inside of each person and every creature, God can also "suffer." He must also run the awesome risk of giving love and being rejected, at least by angels and human beings. This is not a "negative" darkness in God that leads nowhere. There is in God a positive aspect of darkness, of potentiality in what both He and His creatures can become by accepting the undefined, the not-yet, the potential that is at the stirrings of all love movements from the darkness of not-yet to the glorious light of what-could-be.

Such a darkness in God's relationship to His material universe is characterized by the words of Genesis:

> Now the earth was a formless void, there was darkness over the deep, and God's spirit hovered over the water (Gn 1:2).

DARKNESS WITHIN THE TRINITY

I f God relates to His material world not only as the initiating First Cause, but also in an aspect of a potential Father recognized and loved into new relationships by His human children, it is because within the very one nature of God, shared equally by three distinctive, personal relationships of Father, Son and Holy Spirit, there exists also a giving and a potential to receive in love.

Before the Father can be a realized relationship toward the Son in the love of the Spirit, there exists in the Godhead what Meister Eckhart called the Abyss, the Desert, the wilderness, prior to movement. This Godhead is "motionless unity and balanced Stillness and is the Source of all emanations."[5] Godhead does not yet describe a Mind that speaks a Word and thus becomes a Mind by such a thinking-love action. There is fullness of being, but silence is what is before the Father hears Himself speak His Word. Such indeterminateness is not negativity, or absence of being. It is the fullness of richness and beyond all classification of being.

But out of this dark Void of utter richness there stirs a movement "outward," towards Another. The dark side of God's *no-thingness* turns to light as God wishes to find Himself in self-giving to His Word. Thus, out of the darkness of unrealized potentiality in self-giving, the

Father becomes Father and finds His true personhood in not only giving Himself to His Son but in being retrieved from *non-beingness* to being the Father of the Son.

Now God has a name, Father, because His meaningfulness is expressed in His self-giving to His Son through His Spirit of Love. God would always have remained the Void had it not been through the stirring of the Spirit of Love to call the Father out of the darkness into the light through His love given to and returned by His Son.

Jesus Christ revealed while on earth this essential mystery of the Father communicating Himself to us through the Son and the Spirit. "To have seen me is to have seen the Father . . . I am in the Father and the Father is in me" (Jn 14:9, 10). He also revealed that only through the Holy Spirit can we come to know the Son and all He is to the Father. "When the Advocate comes whom I shall send to you from the Father, the Spirit of truth, who issues from the Father, he will be my witness" (Jn 15:26; also Jn 14:17, 26; 16:14).

There can be no Father, therefore, but as revealed in the light of the loving relationships to the Son and Spirit. There can be no Son relationship except in relation to the Father that begets Him eternally, that calls the Word out of the Void of silence into an expressed Image of His very own Mind as a fathering Mind. And such a begetting and being a begotten cannot be possible except as manifested through the Spirit that broods over the Void as the Spirit of Love.

There could be no Father, but only Darkness in reference to the possibility of such an identity, until the Godhead moves to know Himself in His image, His Son. The Father thus becomes the knower and the Son is known, but also vice versa, the Son in the Spirit is the knower as He knows the Father to be His total Source and Origin of being. And the Father is known as Father. But this movement from darkness to light, from possibility to actualized relationships as Father and Son, can come about only through the Holy Spirit in love. The Spirit makes it possible that the Father and Son mutually know themselves and mutually to affirm themselves as Father and Son and mutually to recognize themselves as such. The Father and Son, knowing themselves in that primal act of "emptying" of the Father into the Son and the Son "emptying" of Himself into the Father in mutual self-surrender is nothing but the binding force of the Holy Spirit as Love.

Through this threefold movement in light all reality within the Trinity and in the order of creation flows. Toward us we are called from darkness and potentiality into the light of our true identity only by means of God's uncreated energies of love.

Still, as the total God in one essence condescends to touch us in His energies of love, there is also a darkness in God. God the Father is not yet totally called out of darkness into the light of actuality as *our* Father. Nor is Jesus Christ totally accepted by us as light but we permit darkness to exist in Him since we fail to live in Him as His dynamic members. The Spirit is hidden in the dark potential of possibly actualizing us as loving children of the Father in His Son until we consent to surrender to His guidance.

How can we ever know that God in His relationships with us can exhibit a form of "incompleteness," a desire to receive our love; that in any way God is vulnerable and can suffer if we resist to return His great love? We can know nothing of the trinitarian relations, about the Father, Son and Holy Spirit, except through God's Word made flesh, Jesus Christ.

GOD'S DARKNESS IN JESUS

God's darkness becomes revealed for us, becomes a transfigured light, through the darkness in Jesus. We have no way of learning about the suffering love within the heart of the Father except that we see the heart of Jesus pierced and emptied totally for love of us. "To have seen me is to have seen the Father" (Jn 14:9).

The terrifying sufferings, the extreme darkness of complete rejection and abandonment that Jesus underwent in His human life, especially on the cross, is a powerful statement about God. It is not a logical statement. It is an intuition granted to the *anawim*, the little ones in God's Kingdom, who are not scandalized by God's darkness.

> For God's foolishness is wiser than human wisdom,
> and God's weakness is stronger than human strength (1 C 1:25).

Jesus had told St. Paul God's secret: "My power is at its best in weakness" (2 C 12:9). God is always God, unchangeable in His essence as the Beginning and the End of all reality. But God's pursuing love for us, His vulnerable waiting for our response, His "pathetic" or suffering love becomes revealed and manifested to us in human terms when Jesus unfolds through His sufferings in darkness His burning love on the cross for us.

Nowhere is God more God than in the revelation of Jesus as broken and rejected, "A worm and not a man" (Ps 22:6). In the self-emptying and total surrender of Jesus to His Father on our behalf we are at last able to enter into the trinitarian community and there discover also something of a similar darkness in the eternal relationships of the Father, Son and Holy Spirit toward us. God's so great love for us (Jn 3:16) can only be seen in the crucified Jesus. He does not suffer and die alone. But He is the image of the invisible God (Col 1:15), the concrete expression of what is always going on with the Trinity.[6]

A SUFFERING GOD

Does God watch Jesus die and still remain "immutable" and eternally unchanging? Is the heart of God so unfeeling and stoical that there is no suffering love that flames forth at the sight of Jesus who was despised and rejected by men (Is 53:3)? Does Jesus alone enter into the black darkness of temptation and rejection or does He image for us also the readiness of the Father to suffer for all of us? God flashes forth in that darkness on the cross as a flaming meteor of love, ready to go to the ultimate in giving Himself to us. God is mostly God when the brokenness of Jesus on the cross shouts out to us: "God is like this!"

God is light. But Jesus' sufferings tell us that God is also darkness. He is love that is patient; endures all things (1 C 13:4, 7). What kind of a love would God have for us if He were not ready to suffer and lay down His life for us (Jn 15:13). But the Good News is that God does love us as Jesus does. "As the Father has loved me, so I have loved you" (Jn 15:9). Jesus images the love of the Father for us in His brokenness and rejected condition.

But unless we realize that in some mysterious but real way the Father also suffers as Jesus suffers, the love of God may remain abstract and uninvolved. It could be a detached Platonic love for us, but would it be love strong enough to drive the darkness of self-centeredness out of our hearts by the light of the Spirit's illumination? This is truly a mystery that can be accepted only by the gift of the Spirit's faith.

A SUFFERING FATHER

C an we believe that the Heavenly Father, looking upon the terrify-ing sufferings of Jesus as He is engulfed by the waves of darkness and desolation, abandonment and seeming rejection, not only by His people but by His own Father who had earlier throughout His human existence of Jesus manifested an involved, infinite love for Him, did not in some way also suffer? Can we not also accept the Father as a Suffering Servant on our behalf? We must reject anything that would resemble the 3rd-4th century heresy called "Patripassi-anism," that held that the Father also underwent the passion in the form of Jesus' body. But by approaching darkness as a part of an unrealized relationship in love, we can perhaps believe that the Father also along with the Spirit is involved in actual suffering with Jesus on our behalf.

The darkness in the Father is not the identical darkness suffered by Jesus. Yet the Father suffers as the potential Father as He sees His Son suffer in His unique darkness. If human fathers can suffer at the sight of their sons suffering, why should the Father not suffer as the Father of Jesus sees His Son emptied on the cross for love of us? A Father that could not suffer would be no Father. A God that could not suffer out of love would be no holy, good and beautiful God.

When Jesus entered into the darkness of abandonment and shrieked out: "My God, my God, why have you deserted me?" (Mk 15:34), the emptying of the Suffering Servant of Yahweh reached its peak. But so also did the emptying of the Heavenly Father in the total binding love of the Spirit of that Father with His Son and with all of us. Never was there more manifested in human language and history the God of darkness, stretching out in vulnerability to possess the return of our love than at that moment of Jesus dying on the cross.

And yet strangely to tell, that darkness in the Father is turned to light as the depths of the Spirit's love is manifested to the Father in

Jesus' human brokenness. The Father's suffering is turned to joy as He must have uttered those beautiful words that He spoke at Jesus' baptism: "This is my Son, the Beloved; my favor rests on him" (Mt 3:17; Mk 1:11; Lk 3:22).

Still, not all is light in the Father as the Son is glorified just as Jesus does not totally lose His darkness and brokenness in his "passover" to the new creation. Both the Father and the Son in the Spirit of love stretch out towards us in a similar darkness and suffering. The Father still is pained at seeing the members of the Body of His Son suffering. This darkness continues as long as any of us human beings insist on remaining in our darkness by not accepting God's love for us.

Gerald Vann, O.P. articulates this mystery of the suffering God in our time-perspective in these words:

> But in the life of God there are no events; God has no history. Eternity is not an endless line running parallel with the line of time; it is a point; and what to us is past or future is as much present to eternity as is the actual moment we are now living . . . Thus the very immutability of God is not a denial of his involvement in the sorrows of these present times, but a triumphant vindication of it. Of the human body of Christ you can say that first it suffered, and then it was glorified and made glad; but throughout that temporal sequence the Godhead remains unchanged, and unchanged precisely in its knowledge and willing of, and its will to share in, that which Christ on the Cross took to himself and made his own and in his glorification turned into glory.[7]

EVERLASTING LOVE

God is love. And love is not only glory and light. It is also darkness and waiting. As we suffer to the degree that we love when our love or ourselves are not accepted in return love, so God, love by nature, must be always in a state of being ready to suffer. And we know how often we fail to return love to Him and actuate that suffering in God.

God surely does not suffer as we, but suffers nonetheless according to His mode of loving. The cross shows us an infinite love suffering the ultimate that can be described in human brokenness. And yet, even as we stand on Calvary, bathed in the swirling darkness, we are led to believe that not even the human expression of that divine suffering love for us can ever capture fully in any given moment of insight how much God both loves us and suffers on our behalf.

Jurgen Moltman captures something of the Father's suffering different from that of the Son, yet, nevertheless, a real suffering:

> The Son suffers dying, the Father suffers the death of the Son. The grief of the Father here is just as important as the death of the Son. The Fatherlessness of the Son is matched by the Sonlessness of the Father, and if God has constituted himself as the Father of Jesus Christ, then he also suffers the death of his Fatherhood in the death of the Son.[8]

Suffering the loss of His Fatherhood as He sees His Son dying, the Father enters into a "dark" relationship of pained love, given to us out of the depths of His nature as Father to Jesus and also to us who have eternally been destined to be a part of Jesus. This is the "hidden wisdom of God" (1 C 2:7) that St. Paul preached as wisdom of the spiritually matured. Such darkness is a light when we yield to God's suffering love. It gives glory to God in His humble love unto death for us. We, too, enter into His glorious light and live no longer in darkness. Then we will understand the revealed words:

> We teach what scripture calls: the things that no eye has seen and no ear has heard, things beyond the mind of man, all that God has prepared for those who love him (1 C 2:9).

A VALENTINE HEART

St. Valentine's Day
A day for lovers
to remember
that love means death,
that love means a giving
of self to another

who becomes more important
than to your own self.

This is a day to recall
the heart of you, O my God.
No one has ever loved
as You love me.
No one has ever suffered
so much in pained heart
as You who have given me
all in the love of Jesus emptied.

O Jesus!
Yours is the heart
closest to the heart of the Father.
Your pierced and empty heart
mirrors for me the self-emptying
of the Father's love for me.
He knows in You
that love is pain.
It is suffering.
It is death.
It is self-forgetting.
It is living for the other.
It is truly a pierced heart,
emptied of all from within.

O, Father and Son,
pour into my heart
Your humble Spirit
of gentleness and patience,
of love, peace and joy,
that I, too, may learn
to love with Your love
the other selves, my true selves
that You have gifted me
to love as I love myself.

May my heart offered to them
become a pierced heart,
a suffering heart,
as I slowly learn that love is death
but it is also true life!

CHAPTER TWO

BROKENNESS IN JESUS

O ne very basic problem that has perplexed all human beings of all ages has been that of evil and suffering. Job bends in faithful submission to the God of mystery. Ivan Karamazov in Dostoievsky's novel, *Brothers Karamazov*, wishes to return his ticket of admission if God is not righteous and refuses to alleviate innocent suffering.

The great revelation about the God of Israel, that made the God of Jesus so completely different than all the other gods of other religions, was that He was also a suffering God. He promised to go among His suffering people and suffer with them. He would be with them in the Tent of the Meeting, sharing in all of their victories and defeats, joys and sorrows, health and in suffering.

How powerfully this is brought out in the novel, *Night*, of Elie Wiesel, the Jewish survivor of Auschwitz:

> The SS hanged two Jewish men and a youth in front of the
> whole camp. The men died quickly, but the death throes
> of the youth lasted for half an hour. 'Where is God?
> Where is he?' someone asked behind me. As the youth
> still hung in torment in the noose after a long time, I heard
> the man call again, 'Where is God now?' And I heard a
> voice in myself answer: 'Where is he? He is here. He is
> hanging there on the gallows . . .'[1]

GOD IN JESUS

W here is God now? We Christians can say: "God is now hanging on the cross on Calvary, poured out as spilt blood unto the last drop for love of us." Jesus is the perfect image of how much our

Heavenly Father loves us. But He is more. An image often can imply for us an exact duplicate, a static reproduction, as an image in a mirror is there reproduced when the original person stands before it.

We need in a prayerfulness through deepening faith to see the bro' 'enness in Jesus, not only as an exact image of what is in someway found in God, but as a dynamic revelation of Jesus progressively from the first moment of His birth until His last earthly gasp as He becomes that image by His creative suffering.

There are many ways of service and suffering out of love for another human being or for God. We can serve another, even enduring great pain, for a price. People labor unto exhaustion for wages. We can put up with much, as Jesus surely did, in doing whatever God or our friends wish us to do.

But Jesus, at the peak of His complete emptying on the cross, shows us a love that is free and creative. It is spontaneously given with the burning desire to give even more, all because He has progressively experienced the perfect love of His Father. For me this alone explains the ''folly of the cross.'' Jesus on the cross, emptied of all desires except to give more for love of us in the direct intercession before the face of His Father, reaches the peak of a lifetime of growth in self-emptying.

St. Paul reproduces what probably was a liturgical hymn used in some of the early Christian communities in his letter to the Philippians. He sums up the progressive emptying of Jesus in the Greek word, *kenosis*.

> His state was divine,
> yet he did not cling
> to his equality with God
> but *emptied* himself
> to assume the condition of a slave,
> and became as men are;
> and being as all men are,
> he was humbler yet,
> even to accepting death,
> death on a cross.
> But God raised him high

and gave him the name
which is above all other names
so that all beings
in the heavens, on earth and in the underworld,
should bend the knee at the name of Jesus
and that every tongue should acclaim
Jesus Christ as Lord,
to the glory of God the Father (Ph 2:6-11).

A SUFFERING SERVANT

J esus, the radiant Light of the reflected glory of the Father from all eternity, consented to assume the condition of Adam and all other human beings, who by sin became slaves to their own selves. Jesus, however, did not hold on selfishly to His divine nature, but, precisely because He was divine, He surrendered that divine nature, that is always loving in self-sacrifice. Adam failed to become what God had destined him to be—a loving child of God by grace. He strove to possess his human nature as though he were a god.

But Jesus takes on the form of a suffering servant. He enters into our darkened world. He consents not to claim His natural, divine right to rule over the whole world, but to gain it from His Father by debasing service in humble love for us unto the cross. Jesus not only teaches the world but He lives out this basic truth that possessiveness of life, things, other persons, and even of God, destroys while only true love shown in total self-giving heals, liberates and brings happiness that will last forever.

Such is the way of Jesus. But it is His way and His life because it is the way of His Father. This God loves us with a passion, the passion of Jesus. In Jesus' total submission to the point where He possesses nothing of His own to prove His love for us, Jesus is showing us the Father's infinite love.

When Jesus became a weak child, He was unveiling the weakness of God, ready to dispossess Himself of His life in order to share it totally with us. God's weakness is the power He places into our hands to call Him Father. We can hurt Him just as Jesus submitted to hurts and rejections when He offered His love to human beings and received abuse and indifference.

A HEALER OF BROKENNESS

J esus pursued the sinners. He drove out the evil spirits of despondency and loneliness by His involving self-giving to the broken ones of this earth. He tenderly touched the lepers, the paralytics,
the blind and the lame and gave them new life. He entered into the
brokenness of human existence. The evils of the physical and moral
orders surrounded Him from all sides. Such darkness sucked Him
deeper and deeper into its darkness like quicksand. Down into the
dregs of society Jesus entered "to be made sin for us."

The broken ones of this earth clawed at Him. As soon as He looked
for rest in order to escape from human brokenness in order to be one
with the full healthiness of His Father, they brought Him more of the
diseased to be healed. Jesus touched human evils.

Jesus stretched out His hands of healing and the sick felt the love of
God pour into their broken bodies, minds and hearts. He was the Son
of God and they, for a brief moment, hung suspended between the
darkness of their own isolation and the light of the truth that they too
were sons and daughters of God. They yielded to the presence of
Jesus' love in their lives and they felt wholeness come over them.

But before He entered into the darkest of human brokenness in His
passion and death on the cross, Jesus acted out His great mission of
being the image of the Heavenly Father who lives to love us by serving
us. While the disciples fought for the first place closest to Jesus, He
wished to teach them that the greatest in the Kingdom of God are those
who are humble and serve out of love for such is the Father (Lk
22:25-26). Alone with His friends, Jesus in the upper chamber opens
His loving heart to them. It is a humble heart that wants to serve as a
slave. Jesus bends down and washes the feet of Peter and John, Judas
and the other disciples. The heart of God never bent down lower to
touch His children than in that gesture of humble service.

> If I, then, the Lord and Master, have washed your feet,
> you should wash each other's feet (Jn 13:14-15).

A GIVING LOVE

H e is one with the Father who loves us by sending His Son, Jesus,
to act out in human gestures that love is service. It is emptying of

self. It is losing in order to find. It is not only to be touched by all the filth and sordidness of a world that groans together in its resistance to fulfillment (Rm 8:22). It is love that seeks actually to be broken like bread is broken in order to be the food of love to nourish the other into true being.

When Jesus took simple bread at the Last Supper and a cup of wine, He symbolically was offering Himself on our behalf with the fullness of love that seeks to give of one's total being. He symbolically was offering Himself unto death and the outpouring of His blood to the last drop. On the next day He lived out His symbolic gestures.

He entered into the depths of His being and pushed Himself to ever greater levels of love for us. He consented to be exposed to the fullness of evil and brokenness as He entered into hidden areas of darkness. He is physically stripped of His clothes, but over the hours on the cross He is stripped of all of His own possession of His life. Love is emptying and on the cross Jesus gives up all self-imposed limits as He pours out His very life as love.

> Harshly dealt with, he bore it humbly,
> he never opened his mouth,
> like a lamb that is led to the slaughter-house,
> like a sheep that is dumb before its shearers
> never opening its mouth (Is 53:7).

Jesus reaches the peak of mirroring forth the suffering, serving Father on our behalf in freely wanting to give Himself and His very life for our sakes. He is not a victim of circumstances turned over to the wiles of men who persecute Him. God's plan, so different from the wisdom of philosophers, would be to touch the hearts of us human beings by suffering and being broken before our eyes.

> And yet ours were the sufferings he bore,
> ours the sorrows he carried.
> But we, we thought of him as someone punished,
> struck by God, and brought low.
> Yet he was pierced through for our faults,
> crushed for our sins.
> On him lies a punishment that brings us peace,
> and through his wounds we are healed (Is 53:4-5).

Becoming like "water draining away" (Is 22:14), Jesus enters into the darkness of abandonment that came over His human consciousness. As He pushed deeper into that darkness, through spaces even of His unconscious, hitherto unexplored, Jesus stretched out to discover His loving Father's face that so often before in His earthly life was shining His approving, supportive love. Now He sinks into a void where He confronts His last and greatest temptation.

Earth, sky and air suddenly froze in a mute stare at the white figure hanging on the cross. His cry pierces the darkened silence:

> My God, my God, why have you deserted me?
> How far from saving me, the words I groan!
> I call all day, my God, but you never answer,
> all night long I call and cannot rest (Ps 22:1-2).

DARKNESS UNTO DEATH

I n that cry Jesus becomes every broken human being that has ever doubted whether God really cared. He, who was continuously surrounded by the love of the Father, now finds Himself alone in complete darkness. Not even a ray of light, a crack opening to hope that the Father still loved Him was near to grasp onto and for Him to be led out of the agonizing confinement of "aloneness."

The prophet Jeremiah had caught something of this apparent rejection Jesus would feel in His dark sufferings on the cross.

> Now a storm of Yahweh breaks,
> a tempest whirls,
> it bursts over the head of the wicked;
> the anger of Yahweh will not turn aside
> until he has performed and carried out,
> the decision of his heart.
> You will understand this in the days to come (Jr 30:23-24).

Fear, doubt, rejection pour over Jesus in His last hour. He pushes to new levels of loving abandonment, of dispossession of Himself and His very own life itself. "Do not stand aside, Yahweh. O my strength, come quickly to my help" (Ps 22:19). The Father can reject Him. But still He will love Him. Where are you, God? Why do you not hear me and come to help me? Remove this suffering. Destroy me, but don't say you do not love me.

In such ultimate brokenness of body, soul, spirit, Jesus moves humanly into a consciousness of self-emptying love that has been His from all eternity as His "natural" response to the Father's total gift of Himself to His Son. As the soft, velvety fingers of morning dawn gently lift the darkness from the face of the earth to let the sun burst into being with full radiance, so the light of the Father's love softly falls upon His broken spirit to drive away the darkness of despair and abandonment.

> For he has not despised
> or disdained the poor man in his poverty
> has not hidden his face from him
> but has answered him when he called (Ps 22:24).

MY BELOVED SON

Jesus hears words that only He could hear. "You pleased Me, My Son. I do love you and all I have is yours. I was absent only that you might seek Me. Now we are one forever in the glory of My love for you that can never know another moment of darkness." Although that hill seemed to the passers-by a bit of earth never more destined to see the sun warm its breast, yet the broken Jesus had passed slowly from darkness to the soft rays of spring morning. The scent of flowers heavily laden with nectar and the promise of seeds unto a hundredfold filled His nostrils. He was alive!

> I was dead and now I am to live
> forever and ever,
> and I hold the keys of death
> and of the underworld (Rv 1:16).

From brokenness to life; from darkness unto light. Jesus is Victor! And this life eternal He wishes to share with us in our brokenness!

MEDITATION

Into our broken world
You came, Lord Jesus.
You embraced our darkness,
even though You are pure light.
You were born in a cave
and wrapt in flimsy cloth,
You who cover the heavens with the sun, moon and stars.
You cried for Your mother's milk,
You who feed the entire world.
You needed the warm arms of a mother,
You who stretch out to embrace the universe.
You submitted to the Law,
You who make all laws of nature.
You were baptized as a sinner in the Jordan,
You who are sinless and all pure.
You traveled about preaching to the multitudes,
You who are the silent, everlasting Word of God.
You touched the lepers,
gave sight to the blind,
opened the ears of the deaf,
because You came to give them abundant life.

You, the King of the universe,
became like a humble servant.
You were hungry and thirsty,
You who provide food and drink for all.
Sinners touched You
and were healed of their loneliness.
You were called a friend of harlots
You the pure Bridegroom of Your Church.
You were poor with no pillow for Your head,
You who possess the fullness of the Father.

You were the light,
but the darkness did not comprehend.
You offered love,
but received rejection in turn.

You wept for the sins of the world,
You, the Joy of the world.
You washed the feet of sinful men,
the Master who came to serve.
Ours were the sufferings You bore,
ours the sorrows You carried.
You were struck low
as a criminal, crushed for our sins.
You were acquainted with sorrows,
You who brought pleasure to Your Father.
Your sufferings and punishment
bring to us peace and forgiveness.
And by Your wounds
      we can be healed.

O, Jesus, radiant Light,
You entered into our darkness
of sin, violence and shame,
that we might have a share
      in Your healing light.
On the cross, like a valiant warrior,
You entered into the battle
of light against darkness,
of love against selfishness,
of giving against possessing.

The soldiers looked upon You
      whom they had pierced
for they saw that to break Your bones
was useless for You were total brokenness.
You were taken down from the cross,
wrapt again in flimsy cloth
and held in the arms of Your Mother.

"Jerusalem, Jerusalem,
what more could I do for you?"

God has reached the limit
of giving, of self-emptying.
No shade of blackness could be

added to Your darkness.
No more void to absolute Zero!

O God, in Jesus may I learn
that love becomes fiery light
only in the total broken darkness.

CHAPTER   THREE

TEMPTED AS WE

G od's nature is holy. What does true holiness of God mean? What
does it mean that you and I are called "to be holy and spotless and
to live through love in His presence" (Ep 1:4)? Too often our concept
of holiness is tied to anemic-looking Saints who never dared to smile
while on earth or statues like that of St. Joseph, always holding a
never-wilting lily.

To describe God's holiness is to touch the "insideness" of God.
God's power can be seen in His creative works of nature. But God's
holiness is God in His perfection as good and beautiful and loving. It
is, above all, God in the totality of His being, moving outwardly
towards the other, towards man and angel, to offer Himself as gift. In
Holy Scripture, whenever God is described as holy, He is always close
to man or angel, involved in a communicating of His loving nature
unto communion, so that His perfection may be shared in a union of
love (Lv 11:44-45).

Isaiah was swept up in a vision before the throne of God and heard
the Seraphs crying out constantly: "Holy, holy, holy is Yahweh
Sabaoth" (Is 6:3). Moses fell back before the holiness of Yahweh in
the burning bush. For that was *holy* ground (Ex 3:4-6) because God is
holy and He made Himself present in self-giving in that place. His
holiness was localized in the Ark of the Covenant and in the Holy of
Holies in the Temple for it was there that Yahweh promised to enter
into His special, loving communication with His people.

God's holiness is, therefore, God in loving, self-giving relationships with us in order that we may share most intimately in His very
own life (2 P 1:4). This is our end: ". . . be holy in all you do, since it is
the Holy One who has called you, and scripture says: Be holy, for I am

holy'' (1 P 1:15-16). God calls us to receive His holiness and to
become holy as He is, to open ourselves to His outpouring love and
gift of Himself for us and then to become outpoured gift in love of Him
and neighbor. We are called to be saints, or holy people, sanctified by
God's holiness incarnate through His Holy Spirit. "We have been
called by God to be holy, not to be immoral" (1 Th 4:7). God chose us
from the beginning to be holy by the sanctifying power of the Holy
Spirit (2 Th 2:13).

JESUS BECOMES HOLY

I f Jesus is God made flesh who dwells among us (Jn 1:14), then our
idea of Him as holy is that He always was holy. He could not sin.
But this is to refuse that He was also *human*. Jesus comes to act out
God's holiness. God's holiness will be like the holiness of Jesus. But
this holiness comes to us, is revealed or manifested to us only through
the actions and words and person of the human Jesus. When Jesus was
baptized by St. John the Baptist in the Jordan, the Evangelists likened
it to Jesus' anointing, His baptism by the Father's Spirit of love. St.
Mark repeats words found in prophecy of the Old Testament: "Thou
art my Son, my beloved; with thee I am well pleased" (Mk 1:11). God
the Father is to be pleased by Jesus because He would grow into
becoming the Servant of the Lord, the suffering Servant, the *Ebed
Yahweh*. "Behold my servant . . . my chosen, with whom I am well
pleased" (Is 42:1). ". . . the Lord has laid on him the iniquity of us
all" (Is 53:6).

Jesus throughout His whole life, in cooperation with the Holy
Spirit, had to strive to become holy. In the Last Supper, Jesus prays to
His Father:

> As you sent me into the world,
> I have sent them into the world,
> and for their sake I consecrate myself
> so that they too may be consecrated in truth (Jn 17:18).

We must not think that Jesus had to receive the Spirit whom He did
not already possess and, therefore, that He was not eternally God. In
His experiences, especially through His temptations, Jesus had to

discover and manifest the Spirit that belongs to Him, whom He possesses as His very own Spirit. "He whom God has sent utters the words of God, for it is not by measure that he (God) gives (him) the Spirit" (Jn 3:34; cf. also Is 11:2 and Jn 1:33).

JESUS TEMPTED

J esus was driven into the desert by the Holy Spirit (Mk 1:12) and there He was tempted. He was tempted all His lifetime also, "like us in all things save sin" (Heb 4:15). "Now you know that he appeared in order to abolish sin, and that in him there is no sin; anyone who lives in God does not sin . . ." (1 Jn 3:5-6). Jesus was sinless because He yielded to God's Spirit within Him and went against any urge toward independence. We see from the Synoptic accounts of Jesus' temptations in the desert how the early Christians testified to their belief that Jesus progressed in holiness by overcoming temptations (Mt 4:1-11; Mk 1:13; Lk 4:1-13). There have been many attempts by biblical exegetes to explain the desert temptations. At least, as we read the Synoptic accounts, we realize, as essential to the truth revealed, that He had to struggle within His heart to reach the state of loving, humble submission to His Father that eventually would mean His ignominious death on the cross.

It is impossible to ponder how the Evangelists arrived at this reconstruction of what clearly seems to bear the imprint of an actual experience lived through by Jesus, even though the struggle may not have been an incident that happened only once in the very way as it was narrated. Jesus would grow in holiness as He fought the Prince of Darkness for dominance both in His own life and in the lives of those He healed from demonic possession. His struggle would end only on the cross when He would be lifted up and His adversary then would definitely be thrown down from his throne and stripped of his power.

The holiness of Jesus is seen not only as the presence of the Father's Spirit in the Son of Man giving Him strength to unmask and defeat the Devil but also as a growth process which brings holiness to Jesus as He confronts the Evil One and conquers him. The three temptations highlight Jesus' total attachment to His Father. Jesus is given temptations much as Eve, the *anima* symbol of what is in all

of us, underwent in the Garden, to take the initiative in His hands in
an aggressiveness that would deny God's sovereignty over Him. He
would not yield to feed Himself by anything but by God's word.
Power and glory over humble worship to God were rejected by Jesus'
quotation from Deuteronomy 6:13. "You must worship the Lord your
God, and serve him alone" (Lk 4:8). Finally, He claims His divine
origin, not by presuming on God's power to protect Him, but by an
inner poverty of spirit that puts His whole dependence upon God's
goodness. "You must not put the Lord your God to the test" (Lk
4:12).

ABANDONMENT TO GOD IN DARKNESS

The Gospels present the peak of Jesus' holiness as an *exodus*
experience. He was tempted in His growth in holiness to hold on
to His own life rather than to surrender His life on behalf of sinful
mankind. Imaging the Father's holiness in His own human develop-
ment, Jesus grew in each event as He sought to do, not His own, but
His Father's will. "Here I am! I am coming to obey your will" (Heb
10:9). Jesus saw certain ways of acting as coming under His Father's
commands and these He freely accepted to accomplish, even when it
meant His death on the Cross (Lk 22:42).

His holiness prompted Jesus to a joyful response to do all that His
human consciousness revealed to Him as falling within the area of the
Father's wish, or even more sensitively, what would please His Father
more. He could say that His holiness drove Him always to "do what
pleased him" (Jn 8:29). It is the terrifying abandonment by His loving
Father on the cross that becomes for Jesus His last and greatest
temptation (Mk 15:34). Unlike the surrender of Himself in the desert
and the Garden of Gethsemane where He is consoled by the Father's
presence of an angel, on the cross darkness yields to more darkness.

Jesus, who had tested the joys of loving His Father, now tastes
only a seeming hostility of the Father towards Him. He who was
without sin, "for our sake God made the sinless one into sin" (2 C
5:21). Here do the love and holiness of Jesus for His Father shine forth
in darkness. The *light* of God's holiness appears to us in the darkness
of the awful temptations of Jesus on the cross. This must have
consisted in the terrifying questioning in the mind of Jesus about the

Father's love for Him and why the Father refused to manifest Himself in love to Him in His great dark hour. Jesus seems to be rejected cruelly by His Father. Yet He remains faithful in the temptations that cross His mind. Holiness ultimately is total surrender to God, even if God seemingly rejects the gift.

In this, His greatest temptations, Jesus is tempted to doubt, in the absence of the Father's loving approval, His own identity. Perhaps the crowd gazing up at Him while He hangs on the Cross is right after all. "If you are God's son, come down from the cross." (Mt 27:40). Yet in spite of His temptations, Jesus pushes to new depths of holiness and loving surrender as He cries out: "Father!" He still gives Himself as gift even though the Father does not seem present to receive it or even seemingly cares about the gift. In that struggle of temptations Jesus attains, in His human expression, the holiness of God. This is the victory of His holiness and it is the crowning in human language of the Trinity's holiness, of self-giving to mankind unto death and complete abandonment.

DRIVEN INTO THE DESERT

The Holy Spirit is always driving us, as He drove Jesus into the desert, to enter into our "hearts", the deepest levels of consciousness and there in utter darkening of our own rational control over God, we are called to enter into the spiritual struggle, the interior combat. It is in such deep areas of our inner being in times of temptations that we are called to become "pure of heart" through the presence of the Spirit of love.

The Church gives us special times, such as the liturgical season of Advent and Lent, in which we can more thoroughly enter into the dark areas of our inner being and there come to grips with our temptations in a very special way that often is not exercised in our daily living. We are to stand with vigilant attention to the interior movements of our hearts in order to see that the great enemy, preventing us from responding generously to God's call to share His divine life, is really, after all, *ourselves* in our self-love or self-centeredness. We do have the "old man" within all of us (Col 3:9; Ep 4:22). There must be an all-out war to exterminate our self-love (1 C 10:6-11). And this is the daily cross that the soldier of Christ is bidden by Him to carry.

Thus self-abnegation, both negative and positive, is absolutely necessary in our lives. There must be a checking, inhibiting, nullifying of the inclinations that gravitate toward self as the center of all of our desires. We need to replace this more positively with God as the center of all our aspirations. Instead of concentrating most of our spiritual efforts on the negative aspects and on legalism, we need to endeavor to transform radically the springs of our daily activities through a movement that comes out of a deep interiority.

THE INNER STRUGGLE

The inner struggle to allow God to become truly God is almost a "white" martyrdom. At times of intense temptations we would gladly pray for a "red" martyrdom that in one fell swoop would be all over, instead of such a slow "burn" of the people around us who get on our nerves, of our own constant failings, especially of our own naive forms of selfish pride shown in dealing with others, especially with God. It is only in such trials and temptations endured with patience and a constant crying out to God to become our protector and stronghold against the enemies' attacks that we truly enter into genuine love and prayer.

Humility is attained only in battle, not from sermons and books. Virtues that build on the foundation of humility or truth are acquired through suffering. Run away from suffering and temptations and you will have no virtues acquired for you will not have put on the mind of Christ. It is truly in suffering that humility is engendered and that you finally love God purely for Himself because He is God. The importance of tribulations in your spiritual life lies in the fact that only through such trials do you acquire true humility. You see clearly the futility of your own efforts and the importance of God becoming your Savior.

FROM DARKNESS TO LIGHT

It is in the state of temptations that you cry out in humility and fear for the face of God. Everything may be very dark, the desert is dry and empty. Light has eclipsed from everything and you feel that you have lost the way. It is in such spiritual ennui or despondency that you feel most your immobility, having been blocked at every exit. Confinement seems to press in from all sides to suffocate you. It would be so much easier to run away or to choose your own type of trial over those that are presented by the Spirit in your unique desert. No one owns your desert! It is all yours and in a way you made it. Have you ever been reduced in temptations to being alone, crying out to God for His infinite mercy, yet thinking that there is no one to hear your cry? In such poverty you begin to believe in your Creator and Savior. You search desperately as you never did before when all was light, for the presence of God as the only source of reality. God is becoming finally God!

The greatest temptation that all of us must undergo, and all through our lives, are those of pride. This is the greatest test of our love, to die to self-love and abandon ourselves totally in love to God. But before we reach, as Jesus did on the Cross, this state of complete surrender of ourselves to God, what hellish thoughts we must pass through! What terrifying thoughts of blasphemy and doubts about God's existence! "How could He really love me?" we find ourselves constantly asking. "Jesus is really not truly God but just a man, and, therefore, God has not yet proved His love for me! God could never forgive my innumerable sins! I am left alone to battle these dark forces! God has forsaken me! He really is not a God of mercy and love but a terrifying God of vengeance and He has discarded me. God really doesn't care anything about me!"

It is in such a state that love is purified and true prayer of total emptiness is reached. Pride is the ultimate temptation that is never really completely conquered while we are on this earth. Desolation allows us to cry out in our state of apparent abandonment. But pride "counsels the soul not to profess God as its helper, but to ascribe to itself its righteousness and to puff itself up before its brethren, considering them to be ignorant because not all of them think so highly of it" writes Evagrius of the 4th century. The greatest thing we can do is to stay in the desert and not return to the flesh pots of Egypt. Stay and do the battle for there is no other way to true life except through the dying that only the desert of temptations and trials bring about when we carry the cross.

TRUE UNION WITH GOD

Much has to be de-mythologized in the Gospels and in the language of the Saints and the ascetical and mystical writers who teach us about the spiritual life and how to attain the goal of all of us, namely, how to advance in greater union with God and neighbor in true authentic love by humble service shown. But the universal teaching of the Old and New Testament is that there is a need for *constant* purification. God does prune the branches to bring forth greater fruit (Jn 15:1). He loves us, His children, and so He disciplines us. But also, there is in all of us much darkness brought on by our own sinfulness and by that of others who have acted upon us to form us into self-centered persons. If we wish to enter into an ever-increasing awareness of loving union with the triune God, then we must expect a life-time of dying to self-centeredness.

The contemplative Christian must surrender to God's complete control on all levels of human existence. This means that the love of God is discovered and experienced to the degree that a person empties himself or herself of all that may impede a total surrender in trusting love to God. This is a movement toward your true self in an ever-increasing integration of yourself in Christ, loved infinitely by a triune God so that you may live now according to that dignity in all of your divine and human relationships. This purifying process is a continued dying to selfishness, to inner darkness and a simultaneous rising, unto light and glory, through a more intense love relationship to God.

True contemplation is loving union in a self-sacrificing community of Father, Son and Holy Spirit that, through purification, allows the contemplative Christian to be godly in the same love and humble service toward all others. Darkness and death can only lead to light and life in the Christian vision where prayer is synonymous with purified love. This is another way of saying there can be no holiness but through self-giving that is brought about in temptations toward unselfish giving. In this sense Lent is every day as we have more and more the courage to be led by the Holy Spirit deeper and deeper into the desert of our selfishness to put to death the false self and to rise in the very desert of our inner poverty to a new richness in Christ, to reach the victory of Easter morning when the desert will yield to us its most cherished secret: ''There is only Christ: He is everything and He is in everything'' (Col 3:11).

MEDITATION

Jesus:
I stand before You,
who are haggard and lean,
from lack of food and drink,
from trials and temptations in the desert.

I see You in the moonlight
as You prostrate in the olive garden,
torn by fear of death,
of suffering so much
for such little avail.

I approach in the darkness
of Your noon ''hour''
and stand beside Your Mother
at the foot of the cross.

You are like a potsherd,
broken, and all spilt out.
''Without beauty, without majesty,''
You are a man of sorrows
familiar with human sufferings.

You truly were tempted,
as we, in all things,
yet You did not sin.

You, the Light of the world,
consented to enter into darkness.
In the struggle to overcome the darkness
around You and within You,
Your holiness became incandescent.
It reached its peak of glory
in the ignominy of Calvary,
when all darkness of self-centeredness
dissolved in the light of Your Father's love.

"My God, my God!"
in darkest abandonment
brought Your victory cry:
"Father, into Thy hands I commend my spirit."

Lord, Jesus, meek and humble of heart,
meet me in my darkest moments,
and, as warm sun gently
scatters darkness and fog,
so come and be my light.

In times of trial and temptation,
be my strength and consolation.
Teach me not to fear the darkness,
but rather draw me to Your light.

For it can only be in such darkness
that You will become my light.
And in Your light,
may I bring the light
of healing love to all I meet.

CHAPTER FOUR

NOT BY BREAD ALONE

O ne of the great theologians of the early Church was St. Gregory of Nazianzus. He laid down a basic principle that has continued application for all of us, regardless of time and place. He insisted that, whatever Jesus did not assume in becoming human, that in no way could be redeemed. He took upon Himself our complete human nature. This means that Jesus had a full human body that grew and developed as our own bodies do. He moved toward a fully developed psyche with memory, imagination and all the emotions found in a well integrated human person. He had an intellect and a will that unfolded and reached maturity in knowledge and love relationships.

But in becoming totally human, Jesus became vulnerable, as we are, to the "human situation" in which He would grow "to maturity and he was filled with wisdom, and God's favor was with him" (Lk 2:40). Jesus became the Messiah ushering into reality the Kingdom of God for all human beings who would humbly accept Him as Lord. But He did this by enduring temptations and all of the existential brokenness that go with becoming a human being.

We must look upon the temptations that Jesus underwent, especially those which He endured in the desert, as not only those of the Messiah that He was to become through those temptations but as those which we Hi; followers are to undergo in order to become His Church. We are tempted continually with the possibility of growing in greater love-union with the Trinity as a result of successful combat with the opposing enemy. The Church made up of us individual, tempted Christians, is constantly under similar attacks or temptations from inimical forces. As Jesus "assumed" such a state of brokenness by submitting to temptations, so we and His Church have been given strength to overcome similar temptations.

We read of various temptations to which Jesus was subjected during His public ministry (Mk 8:11, 27-33; 10:35-40; Jn 2:18-19; 6:15, 30-31; 7:1-9; 12:12-18). But the early followers of Jesus accorded special significance to the desert temptations that in a summary fashion brought together the main elements that Jesus faced in all other of His human temptations. Let us look at His first temptation undergone in the desert in order to gain insight into a basic temptation that all of us (and, therefore, the Church of Christ) face constantly in our human state of incompleteness.

A HUNGRY JESUS

Matthew's account (Mt 4:1-4) of Jesus' first temptation in the desert presents to us a Jesus driven into the wilderness by the Spirit "to be tempted by the devil." After having fasted for forty days and nights, Jesus, we are told, was very hungry. The tempter sought to induce Jesus, if He really were the Son of God, to turn stones into bread.

Commentators generally point out that the essence of the temptation consisted in Jesus being drawn to use His messianic powers to satisfy His basic, human needs and not to trust in His Father to provide for all His needs in more ordinary ways. Surely we can see how Jesus on another occasion taught His followers not to worry excessively about food or drink.

> Do not worry; do not say, "What are we to eat? What are we to drink? How are we to be clothed?" It is the pagans who set their hearts on all these things. Your heavenly Father knows you need them all. Set your hearts on his kingdom first, and on his righteousness, and all these other things will be given you as well (Mt 6:31-33; Lk 12:29-31).

Jesus repulsed the temptation as a misuse of His messianic powers that were to be used as signs to announce that the Kingdom of God was breaking in upon His listeners as Jesus lovingly would use such powers to lead them to the Heavenly Father. In the desert Jesus would not abuse His mission by insisting in self-righteousness that His hunger could be satisfied by His prerogative and equality with His Father to perform a miracle. He turns away from the tempter by quoting from Deuteronomy 8:3: "Man does not live on bread alone but on every word that comes from the mouth of God."

He does not deny that He is the Messiah, but He is that only in being the Word that faithfully expresses the mind of the Father. He would not use His God-given powers in order to take charge to satisfy His personal needs. How humbly Jesus in this scene symbolically shows us that in His humanity during His whole lifetime on earth He strove to live totally to correspond to the Father's wishes. His will was one with that of the Father.

He shows us that He is the Son of God only by seeking to please the Father. In a word, Jesus overcomes any desire to exist and to act independently of His Father from whom He receives all that He is. He is the Son of God, not by power exercised by Himself and for His own needs, but solely because He seeks to please the Father. This is brought out earlier in St. Matthew's account of the heavenly voice at Jesus' baptism: "This is my Son, the Beloved; my favor rests on him" (Mt 3:17).

FEEDING THE HUNGRY

W e can better understand this first desert temptation by linking it up to another similar temptation that Jesus repelled, also in a desert, after He had fed the hungry by performing a miracle multiplying five loaves of bread and two fish to feed over five thousand (Jn 6:5-15). The crowds followed Jesus by boats to Capernaum and there they tempted Jesus to continue to give them miraculous bread from heaven as a sign that He really was the Messiah (Jn 6:30-31). They remembered the prophecy of Yahweh to His people in the desert: "Yahweh your God will raise up for you a prophet like myself from among yourselves, from your own brothers, to him you must listen (Dt 18:15).

Now they became the occasion to tempt Jesus to prove that He was the long-awaited Prophet, the Messiah, the new Moses, who at will could give them bread. If they saw this happening, they would surely believe in His sign. But Jesus refuses to yield to the temptation of wanting to become the Messiah that they wished for in order to have all of their needs miraculously supplied.

Jesus on two accounts repels the temptation, similar to the first desert temptation. He received an anointing by the Father's Spirit to call all men and women to enter into God's Kingdom. They were to enter the Kingdom by means of a *metanoia*, a change of heart, and by faith. The Jews, who followed Jesus to Capernaum, wanted Him to be their powerful king, to restore the House of Israel to former glory. They sought Him as a magician who would usher them into the Kingdom of God without any effort on their part.

Secondly, Jesus received His mission from His Father. His earthly work was to be the Image of the Heavenly Father in human form. Jesus was the "sign" of God's gracious and merciful in-breaking love upon His scattered and suffering poor children. In no way would He abuse His mission among the poor by seeking power and approval from the crowds solely because He had given them material possessions.

SENT FOR THE POOR

Jesus came to show us in His human actions and in His human personage what our Heavenly Father really is like. He insisted:

> No one can come to the Father except through me.
> If you know me, you know my Father too.
> From this moment you know him and have seen him . . .
> To have seen me is to have seen the Father (Jn 14:6-9).

The Father, as Jesus at all times experienced, is an "emptying" Person. He is the Giver of all life. He pours the fullness of divine being into Jesus (Col 2:9) so that Jesus has received everything from the Father (Jn 5:29). He came among the broken ones of this world to show the infinite, healing love of the Father. "He has sent me to bring the good news to the poor, to proclaim liberty to captives and to the blind new sight, to set the downtrodden free" (Lk 4:18).

When His human heart poured out compassionate love for the sick and needy, who were "like sheep without a shepherd" (Mt 9:36), then human beings were meeting the true Messiah who at last was establishing the Kingdom of God. The whole mission of Jesus on earth was to manifest the tender, merciful love of God for His suffering children.

At times such as in the face of these two temptations to multiply bread as a sign of His own personal power, Jesus holds back because He saw clearly that no longer were such miracles true "signs" of His mission to mirror the Father's love for the poor of this world. At other times Jesus would perform such miracles and healings and appeal to them as signs of His oneness with the Father. His primary work, His hour, was to become the fullness of God's communicating, loving presence to mankind. He could not be side-tracked by any vain glory as a miracle worker or healer. He was merely the Suffering Servant of Yahweh, the Word that was being spoken constantly by the Father and that continually reflected perfectly the Mind that spoke that Word.

Yet because He was so much one with the Father, He, as it were, seeing the maimed, the blind, the lepers and the paralytics, the epileptics and the possessed, the sinners bound by hatred for others, by lust and pride, could not but be compassionate, full of mercy and loving as His Father is. Throughout His whole public ministry Jesus imaged His Father's loving concern for His children. He knew what forces of evil were seeking to destroy God's people. And wherever He saw the power of darkness covering mankind, He burned with zeal to bring the light of God's love to destroy the effects of sin.

What He was and what He did, all were for the poor, the oppressed, the afflicted. He lived to serve them in love and not to use them for His own self-centered aggrandizement. He did feed the crowds bread when they were truly hungry (Jn 6:1-4; Mk 6:30-43; Mt 14:13-21; 15:32-39; Lk 9:10-17), but He would not multiply bread for Himself alone to show the tempting evil spirit that He truly was the Son of God or for others who would then have wanted Him to be their type of a king. Jesus wanted such "signs" to serve always not as ends but as means to draw the poor through such signs to their Heavenly Father.

TEMPTATIONS OF THE CHURCH

I f Jesus were so tempted to misuse the powers given Him in His mission, so also the Church and all of us, members of the Body of Christ, are constantly being tempted to do the same. God has given the Church all that it possesses by way of power to "image" the living

Jesus, the Word of God. It is the encounter in historical time and place of the Risen Jesus who still performs His mission of extending the Kingdom of God to the poor through such signs performed with our cooperation. We and the total Church, made of all of us who yield to the Spirit of the Risen Jesus, are called to serve humanity.

As Jesus was concerned with the whole person that He encountered and wanted to bring into total healing, body, soul and spirit levels, so the Church is concerned with the same poor throughout the world to effect a similar total healing on all human levels. One of the great temptations of the Church throughout all of history has been to become so involved with the materiality of ministering Jesus to the poor that leaders of such a Church could become side-tracked by the very means given them to heal the poor.

At times such Church leaders could even veer away from any concern with the physical needs of the poor of this world. In an ultra-spiritual Church, people were "souls" and the Church's mission was to minister only to that facet of human existence, while ignoring the material side of mankind. At other times the Church could become so involved in meeting the material needs of people that it could forget its total mission. Not by bread alone does man live!

Jesus came among the broken persons of this human world. He knew that His whole mission consisted in not satisfying His own desires but in serving the poor. The Church must be always the Church of the poor, the extension of the suffering Jesus into the modern world. And we, as members of His suffering Body, must stretch out toward the poor, those who are such in their body, psychic and also spiritual needs. We do not use the God-given powers within us to satisfy our need toward identity by serving the poor to bring that about. We, as the Church, do not exist only to run hospitals or soup lines in order that we can have the consolation that we are truly part of the Son of the God. We must repel every temptation that seeks to find our identity through using God's gifts for ourselves.

And this can only be done in our pilgrim-condition by repelling such temptations as Jesus did. His mission was to be poor among the poor. "He was rich, but he became poor for your sake, to make you rich out of his poverty" (2 C 8:9). We cannot be rich with God's healing power within us unless we are truly poor, physically as well as spiritually. And the first, essential element in our true poverty, in our existential humility, is to recognize that anything good in us is God's power and gift. Such gifts, as the power Jesus had to turn stones into bread in order to feed Himself when He was hungry in the desert and to multiply bread to feed the hungry crowds, are given to us to serve in love others in need. Only for God's "mission" among the poor are we to spend God's gifts.

Yet we must, as Jesus, be ready to accept ourselves as we are, in the "thrown-into-the-world" situation in which we live. We must learn to accept the possibility in our incompleteness of being tempted, not to be "poor," but, rather, to become "rich" by using such gifts for our own glory.

We must be ready to live in the experience of brokenness and inner poverty that can assume many forms in our temptations to change stones into bread. Each day we experience anxieties at the possibility of losing our sense of established security, fear of the unknown, a general feeling of helplessness before the demands of life, the loss of meaning and isolation. There comes over us daily the great, existential question that echoes down the dark caverns of our consciousness and unconscious: "Who really am I?"

Jesus answered this by submitting totally His radical dependency to His Heavenly Father. The Father was the Source of His being. Jesus knew and reacted honestly to any suggestion to the contrary that everything He had was given Him by the Father to serve the poor, to be used in loving self-sacrifice for others.

We become our true selves in facing such temptations that could suggest that we use God's gifts for ourselves and conquering them with the same response of Jesus: "Man does not live on bread alone but on every word that comes from the mouth of God."

MEDITATION

Heavenly Father!
May Your loving Spirit
drive me deeper and deeper
into the arid, sterile desert
of my inmost being.

And there in prayer and fasting
may I become hungry
to feed upon Your life-giving Word.

God, how often I, too, am tempted
to turn stones into bread,
to take Your freely bestowed gifts
and use them to feed
my false security, to hide behind my true nothingness,
before the Allness of Your loving presence.

Father, in my great need
to assert my identity
before myself, the world and even You,
may I never yield to the temptation
to take Your powers given to me
and use them for my own selfish end.

But may I be rich in my poverty,
enlightened in my darkness,
fed in my hunger
by Your living Word, Jesus.

May Jesus teach me and the Church
how to be poor to serve the poor,
to overcome every temptation to be falsely rich
by misusing Your gifts
given only to lovingly serve Your poor.

In my inner poverty and emptiness
that only the desert can reveal to me,
may I learn that true food
is not power, but only Your Word,
to obey by loving service to others poor.

May Your gift of the Bread of Life,
that You send down upon Your Anawim,
like manna newly fallen from Heaven,
be my strength and that of Your Church
to live by Your Word
in loving service to all the poor.

CHAPTER FIVE

WORLDLY POWER

O ne of the main causes of brokenness in ourselves and in our world that touches us and leads us further into brokenness is our aggressive use of power to obtain our own will. We are born insecure and in need of caressing, warm love. As we develop, we are continually tempted to move by aggressive actions to maintain our insecurities. We really do believe that such insecurities, firmly buoyed up by power, attack or withdrawal, will keep us in our true personhood. Yet our attempts to maintain that "person" by power is to develop an illusion. What we believe is our true self is actually our false self. And power only takes us farther away from true, human maturity.

This maturity can be reached only by a loving humility that accepts our true identity only in God's infinite love. Only in such love can we let go of power and aggressiveness toward others. Such love of God calls us into loving persons in humble service to others.

POLITICAL POWER

J esus entered into the brokenness of the world. He knew what was in the heart of every man. He experienced the insecurities of individuals, of His religious and political leaders that moved toward a false security by means of power. He Himself, as the story of His temptations shows us, underwent throughout His whole adult life the movement toward the possibility that He could attain His true meaningfulness by asserting Himself in worldly power, wealth, honor.

He was born, as all of us, into a nation of people with a history, both of glory and ignominy, of goodness and of low-mindedness. He knew well, from His prayerful study of Holy Scripture, that the prophets had foretold the coming of the Messiah. He, the Anointed One of Yahweh, would restore the House of Israel to glory. All nations would submit to His rule. Jerusalem would be the center of a new order.

Various groups among the Jews of His time interpreted differently the coming of the Messiah. The Zealots saw Him only as a political tool to set Israel free from the Roman oppression. He would be their King (Jn 6:14-15) delivering them from objection, poverty and ignominy. Others saw the Messiah as the one who would usher the new world into being. He would come in glory, signs and wonders, to gather all nations into the New Age (Dn 7:13-14; Mk 8:11-13) with Jerusalem as the center of all other nations.

Still a few, true "Israelites" understood the Messiah as the Suffering Servant of Yahweh, the *Ebed Yahweh*. He, as Deutero-Isaiah foretold, would become a worm and no man, ugly and poured out in His sufferings and by His wounds all human beings would be healed (Is 53:5).

A GENTLE MESSIAH

Jesus knew His Jewish people and their long history of living in exile, under oppression from foreign powers. He knew their hearts. They were a stiff-necked people that had often in their history forsaken Yahweh. When He entered into our world, He received Jewish blood. He grew up a part of this nation. What He did during the temptations in the desert was a model to describe the temptations that He underwent during His whole lifetime. It was the New Testament writers' way of describing how the early Christians conceived Jesus as the new Israel. Like the chosen people, Jesus in the desert of His consciousness was tempted to use power and glory, the tools of the forces of evil, to bring about God's Kingdom.

Yet Jesus knew, as He confronted Himself as the Father's Anointed One, that it was not by power but by a gentle spirit that He would fulfill the eternal plan. He knew that He would have to suffer in humility and loving self-sacrifice. This was God's hidden plan. For God's foolishness is wiser than human wisdom, and God's weakness is stronger than human strength (1 C 1:25).

Jesus came among us to show us in visible, human form what God is truly like. And although God is the omnipotent Creator of the whole universe, the God of Jesus is a gentle suffering God, waiting eagerly and expectantly for our returned love. Jesus turned at all times inwardly and found the Heavenly Father at the core of His being (Jn 14:11).

There Jesus was bathed in the soft, warm light of His Father's tender but strong and eternal love. He knew in that ever-now loving moment that He was sheer gift of the Father. Everything He had came to Him from the Father.

> The Son can do nothing by himself;
> he can do only what he sees the Father doing:
> and whatever the Father does, the Son does too (Jn 5:19)
> I can do nothing by myself;
> I can only judge as I am told to judge . . . (Jn 5:30).

> . . . because I have come from heaven,
> not to do my own will,
> but to do the will of the one who sent me (Jn 7:16).

> Yet I have not come of myself,
> no, there is one who sent me and I really
> come from him . . . (Jn 7:28).

> . . . and that I do nothing of myself:
> what the Father has taught me
> is what I preach (Jn 8:28).

> Not that I care for my own glory,
> there is someone who takes care of that
> and is the judge of it (Jn 8:50).

> And my word is not my own:
> it is the word of the one who sent me (Jn 14:24).

THE BAPTISM OF JESUS

W hen John baptized Jesus in the Jordan, Jesus was acclaiming that He was from above, as His Father expressed His great pleasure in Jesus. Yet Jesus also was acclaiming to the world that He was human. Standing among sinners, to be baptized unto the remission of sins in a conversion back to God, Jesus was professing His solidarity, not only with His Jewish people in their history of sin and guilt, but also with the whole human race.

Although He had no need for repentance, He was repenting *with* and *for* all of us broken and sinful people. He not only came among us and "emptied himself to assume the condition of a slave" (Ph 2:7), but He entered in a very special way into the sinfulness and brokenness of the human race.

Plato tells us that to the degree something is capable of bringing about great good, to that degree also it can be the instrument for great evil. To the degree that Jesus was one with God in holiness and goodness, desiring in human form to express the outpouring love of the Father for all mankind, to that degree He could have, in His humanity, been tempted to turn away from the Father's plan.

The Gospels teach us that Jesus was tempted as we are in all things (Heb 4:12), yet He sinned not. In describing Jesus entering into a state of brokenness and struggle, the Gospel writers show us that all His lifetime on earth Jesus faced the possibility of using His great powers for His own aggrandizement and not in humble submission to His Father.

TEMPTED TO PRESUMPTION

S ymbolic of Jesus' confrontation with Himself as independent of His Heavenly Father is the second temptation that Jesus is described as undergoing in the desert after His baptism.

> The devil then took him to the holy city and made him
> stand on the parapet of the Temple. 'If you are the Son of
> God' he said 'throw yourself down; for scripture says:
>
>> He will put you in his angels' charge,
>> and they will support you on their hands
>> in case you hurt your foot against a stone' (Mt 4:5-6).

Jesus must have struggled, not only in this desert temptation, but throughout His whole earthly existence to do certain actions to prove to Himself or to those who were seeking to know His origin that He was divine. The demonic around Him and within Him, the potential to say *yes* or *no* to His Heavenly Father, set up situations in which He could grow into His true identity. The devil tempted Jesus to do something to prove that He was the Son of God.

If He really were the Son of the Father, He could easily presume therefore that the Father would protect Him in any and all situations. Thus, throwing Himself off the temple parapet would be no danger since God would send angels to protect Him. The devil speaks to Jesus as though He exists alone: "If you . . ." But Jesus says, "Father."

He rejects independent power, pride and presumption by obedience, poverty of spirit and humility. "You must not put the Lord your God to the test" (Mt 4:7). Jesus conquers the demonic forces by yielding completely in loving service to the Heavenly Father.

In the temptation of Gethsemane Jesus would be tempted to run away from His being captured and put to death. He did not want to die, to drink the cup of sufferings and death, but He rose upward toward His Father, as in the desert temptation, to yield in perfect self-surrender and obedience: "Let your will be done, not mine" (Lk 22:42).

Jesus would see His dignity and identity in total gift back to the Father. God the Father could ask anything of Him and He would obey. He was in no position to demand but to obey the Father. He would live in truth, that the Father is greater than He. Jesus would reject the worldliness to perform signs and wonders to boggle the minds of the Jews in order that they would acclaim Him powerful.

His power would come in His gentle surrender of Himself to please at all times His Father. If John the Baptist humbly could confess that Jesus had to increase while he himself had to decrease (Jn 3:30), how much more Jesus understood that He was important only to exalt the Father. His true power that would conquer worldly power would be loving obedience even unto death. Jesus also would conquer the worldliness in us by pouring His same gentle Spirit into our hearts so we too can live by faith, trust in God and in love for each other.

WORLDLY POSSESSIONS

In the final temptation in the desert Satan reveals himself as the ruler of the kingdom of darkness and brokenness. Jesus is tempted to find

His true identity, not in being the Suffering Servant of Yahweh, but in possessing worldly riches, honors and power.

> Next, taking him to a very high mountain, the devil showed him all the kingdoms of the world and their splendor. 'I will give you all these' he said 'if you fall at my feet and worship me.' Then Jesus replied, 'Be off, Satan! For Scripture says:
>
> > 'You must worship the Lord your God, and serve him alone' (Mt 4:8-10).

The temptation that Jesus receives is one to live in the darkness of the present world that is in slavery to the evil forces. Satan is ruler of this kingdom that produces fruit totally different from those who live, as Jesus, in the kingdom of God.

> When self-indulgence is at work the results are obvious: fornication, gross indecency and sexual irresponsibility, disagreements, factions, envy; drunkenness, orgies and similar things . . . those who behave like this will not inherit the kingdom of God. What the Spirit brings is very different: love, joy, peace, patience, kindness, goodness, trustfulness, gentleness and self-control (Gal 5:19-22).

But Jesus repelled the temptation to possess selfishly the riches of this world for the false power they would bring Him. He declared that His kingdom was not of this world (Jn 18:36).

The sign of God's kingdom is a poverty of spirit. Jesus, by living such poverty of spirit, would conquer the worldly kingdom and give power to His followers to live as He did in this new creation.

JESUS POOR

Jesus throughout all His life rejected such a worldly standard of riches and power that fed the false self and brought more brokenness into this already darkened world. As He daily experienced through the Spirit of love poured into His heart the riches of His Father, He lived in the truth which recognized that everything came from the Father and was to be used to glorify Him. Such poverty for

Jesus is a constant, humble recognition of God's sovereignty and free gift of His love. It is a permanent attitude of mind that Jesus assumes toward Himself, His Father and each person that He meets in life. It is poverty that can be called humility. Jesus was nothing; the Father was all. He is meek and humble of heart (Mt 11:29). Jesus surrenders to do whatever the Father wishes Him to do, even unto death.

Satan, however, tempts Him to be independent of the Father's desires. Jesus repulses the temptation, not only by quoting from Scripture that God alone must be served, but throughout His entire life by living poorly. He so lived only because He lived by the inner richness of His Father's continued gift of Himself to Him. Jesus was born poor. He lived poor as a carpenter in a small village and as an itinerant preacher dependent on the good will offerings of others for food and shelter. He was not destitute or heroic in His poverty. He had wealthy friends and could enjoy the gifts offered to Him. But He was absolutely poor because no *thing* possessed Him. He was possessed only by His Father and so He used things only as an external expression of that inner emptiness before the Allness of His Father.

As Jesus lived and taught us to live in the spirit of poverty, so we are to overcome the temptations of Satan to yield to the riches and power of the world by living a life of simplicity and inner truth. Such poverty of spirit recognizes at all time that God is supreme and not we ourselves. Him alone we must serve. All creatures must become means and not ends so that we can use them to praise and magnify God.

What are the temptations from a broken world which daily face us? The more affluent we become the more we are tempted to want more of the world's kingdom. But in yielding to such temptations we bow down and worship the "prince of this world." Everywhere we move in our modern world we encounter the temptation to turn away from serving God to serve ourselves by wanting the riches and the alluring powers of the world.

By living as Jesus did, actually living poorly, we turn away from Satan toward God. We find our richness and security in Him and not in the riches of the world. We gain freedom by becoming passionately indifferent, detached and unpossessing not only of material riches and power but even of honors and all acquisitions that foster pride and self-absorption.

Jesus was poor and detached from material things because He was so completely attached to His Heavenly Father. He leads us into the richness of freed children of God by His humble Spirit.

Remember how generous the Lord Jesus was: he was rich, but he became poor for your sake, to make you rich out of his poverty (2 C 8:9).

HUMBLE SERVICE

J esus spurned the temptation to find His identity in possessing riches by being poor, humble and loving, not only before His Father, but before each human person that He met. Rooted in the self-sacrificing love that His Father poured into His heart, Jesus gave Himself in a similar emptying love for all of us in loving service. "As the Father has loved me, so I have loved you" (Jn 15:9). He did at any given moment whatever was necessary in order to act out the Father's great love that He was constantly experiencing.

He preached and extinguished the darkness in the minds of His listeners. He bent over and touched those broken in body, soul and spirit and called them into new life. He went about doing good to all because God was tempting Him to loving service and not to power and pride. And so we in our broken world are torn between pride, power, riches and poverty, humility and loving service. Our broken situation is healed by yielding to the supremacy of God in loving and joyful submission to please Him. When we live as Jesus did, then truly the scriptural way of describing the new life in Christ is experienced by us as angels appearing and looking after us also (Mt 4:11).

And although the evil forces that tempt us to greater brokenness will return at another time, yet, at the moment of overcoming the temptation confronted, we do experience a new union with God, a new creation and a new entrance into the Kingdom of God.

MEDITATION

GOD ALONE

Lord, Jesus, I too am alone
in the arid desert of my heart.
It is calm, so still.
Yet all is dark.
Suddenly there flashes
from out the tomb of my heart
a light that dances
laughingly, enticingly.
It coaxes and beckons me
to the brink of the precipice.
"Go ahead and jump!"
a voice shouts deep within.
"You are great and can do no wrong.
God is on your side.
What you think is the very way
that God thinks and approves.
Whatever you want
God will give you
        just as you want it."

Another light brilliantly shining
pierces my inner darkness.
This voice is soft and alluring.
Siren-like it casts over the screen
        of my mind's eye
pictures of places far off,
castles and palaces,
songs and dances, food and drink,
clothes and leisure,
honors and glory,
power and might.
"All this is yours if you will
only promise me
a little favor, ever so small.

Serve me as your master,
want no other
and to you I give
all riches, pleasures and happiness."

O God, like Jesus, may I cry out,
"Away, you tempter!
I belong to God
and Him alone I serve.
To follow your glitter and sham
is to be sucked into the mud
of unendless servitude.
Shame and guilt will be my food
as I waste away in prison cell confining."

Only You, O Lord, shall I obey.
In poverty and lowly truth
I shall be lifted up by You
and declared Your loving son
who always pleases You.

CHAPTER   SIX

A BROKEN WORLD

We were meant by God to be happy children of our one Heavenly Father. We were to live in oneness and harmony with all other human beings as brothers and sisters of a large family. The birds and animals, the stars and sun, the waters and the inhabitants of the sea, the earth and its produce were meant to be harnessed by man into a joyful yielding to help man grow into greater love and happiness.

Yet, when we look around us, we see modern man sitting like a very disturbed child in his isolated corner, sick, lonely, angry and shivering from fright. He has forgotten how to communicate with God. He speaks to his neighbor in a monologue of noisy silence. Materialism has dried up his heart and strewn the arid desert with tinsel and baubles, leaving man like a discarded Christmas tree on a dump heap.

T.S. Eliot describes the modern malaise in his *Murder in the Cathedral*:

> Here is no continuing city, here
>   is no abiding stay.
> Ill the wind, ill the time, uncertain
>   the profit, certain the danger.
> O late late late, late is the time,
>   late too late, and rotten the year;
> Evil the wind, and bitter the sea, and
>   grey the sky, grey grey grey.[1]

Robert Heilbroner, the noted economist, has highlighted two pessimistic themes that dominate American conversation. The first is "a loss of assurance with respect to the course of social events" and the second is the "startled awareness that the quality of our surroundings of 'life,' is deteriorating."[2] Today there are roughly 3.6 billion people on planet Earth. By the year 2050 it could reach "a grotesque 20 billion."[3]

Nuclear armament holds out the possibility of total annihilation. More threatening is the fact that poor nations can gain possession of such nuclear weapons and use them as blackmail against the more developed countries. The present crisis over fossil fuel forms of energy dwarfs before the gigantic problem of heat emission produced by all forms of natural energy which could increase the earth's temperature by 50 C., bringing about a condition impossible for human living.

WHAT IS THE DISEASE?

If we add to the ever-increasing physical evils that threaten our human existence the mounting psychological problems of anxiety, fear, loneliness and frustration that plagued all human lives and the moral evils of greed, selfishness, malice, hatred and cruelty, we see a world of people who are rushing into neuroses and very inhuman conditions of life. Psychologists and sociologists have joined forces with ministers of religion to lament the present conditions on the human scene.

But just what is the disease? How did it all happen? Who really is responsible for this present "mess?" Where do we turn to place the blame? Like Adam, we feel the need to be the accuser and so we turn to someone else to shoulder the guilt. But like King David, we have the finger pointed at us, not by the prophet Nathan, but by our own conscience. "Thou art the man!"

Dr. Karl Menninger in his book, *Whatever Became of Sin?*, insists that much of the problem lies in the ignoring of the reality of personal sin and responsible guilt recognized and rectified by all of us. He writes:

> In all of the laments and reproaches made by our seers and
> prophets, one misses any mention of "sin," a word which
> used to be veritable watchword of prophets. It was a word

once in everyone's mind, but now rarely if ever heard.
Does that mean that no sin is involved in all our troubles—
sin with an "I" in the middle? Is no one any longer guilty
of anything? Guilty perhaps of a sin that could be repented
and repaired or atoned for? Is it only that someone may be
stupid or sick or criminal—or asleep? Wrong things are
being done, we know; tares are being sown in the wheat
field at night. But is no one responsible, no one answer-
able for these acts? Anxiety and depression we all acknowledge, and even vague guilt feelings; but has no one
committed any sins?[4]

Fifty-five percent of 20 million Americans said it was not only all
right but it was a duty for American bombers to bomb the small, far
away country of Vietnam. Such action was meant to protect us and,
therefore, the end justified the means! How many Americans even felt
any remorse when Claude Eatherly and his fellow American pilots
dropped the atom bombs on Hiroshima and Nagasaki? Eatherly was
declared a national hero. He became alcoholic, sought to commit
suicide several times and finally was confined to a mental hospital.

We in the United States make up only 6% of the world's population and yet we consume 35% of the world's food and 40% of its total
consumer goods. Millions are starving all over the world and yet we
continue to overeat and dump into the garbage disposals food that
would feed millions. Are we individually concerned that one billion
dollars of our tax money are spent annually to maintain 4,000 prisons
and yet 90% of those prisons are operated in such inhumane manner
that such prisoners will be caught up into a continued web of crime
with little or no rehabilitation resulting from such "corrective"
centers?

The disease is that we have replaced ourselves as the center of our
lives instead of God. A universal *angst* or anxiety fills our hearts with
a sense of meaningless. Our immersion in pragmatic materialism has
suffocated our communion with God's Spirit deeply within our in-
nermost self. Thus cut off from an experienced relationship with God,
the Absolute Transcendent, we are adrift on a dark, stormy ocean that
threatens our very meaningfulness. Not experiencing in deep adora-

tion and worship the pure love of God for ourselves, we find it impossible to be noble and loving toward others. We immediately think of ourselves and our comforts before the happiness and well-being of others, especially if such a concern costs us a price in self-sacrifice.

Without God fear grips us. And yet we use our scientific technology to fight and conquer our fears. Such an approach only increases fears. When we suppress God from our lives and our important decisions that guide our lives toward what we value as a meaningful existence, then we begin to lose our sense as a person.

ADAM, WHERE ARE YOU?

This is the story of Adam, the first man, and of everyman, of you and me. When man placed his own desires and self-directed life outside of God's loving direction, he alienated himself, not only from God but from his own true self and from the human community around him. God, in the mytho-poetic account of man's fall into sin as recorded in the Book of *Genesis*, called out to man, "Where are you?" (Gn 3:9). Man separated himself from God and his sin separated him from the world community.

When we search in Holy Scripture for an account of sin the first question that we find the sacred writers of the Old Testament asking is, not how did sin come into the world, but, rather, how can the sinfulness in their experienced world be explained? The account of the fall of Adam and Eve is not so much a historical account of the first, personal sin of man and woman as it is an explanation of sinfulness as it exists in the world at any time of history through the personal sins that all human beings commit in refusing to give God supreme sovereignty and in breaking solidarity with the human race.

God created man and woman in a loving relationship to Himself and to each other. They were endowed with free will to live in loving union or to disobey God. Yet they chose to be their own masters. Scripture describes the result of sin as a violation of God's established order. Man flees as an exile from God. But he also runs away from his true self that can only be attained in loving union in a community with others.

The *Genesis* account is telling us that sin first entered into the human race by man freely breaking the social oneness that he was meant to enjoy with God and with other human beings. Original sin is more than the first, personal sin of the first human being, that is then juridically imputed to every human being thereafter born into the human race. It is that first sin and each personal sin of every other human being that has ever lived, including you and me. But it adds the oneness of an alienated human community, separated from each other through an inability to love each other because of a "bias" toward self, yet all united in their selfishness. We are all united in our broken condition and alienation from God and from each other and from the material cosmos.

A. Hulsbosch well describes the meaning of original sin in terms of community solidarity:

> Original sin is the powerlessness, arising from nature, of man in his incompleteness as creature to reach his freedom and to realize the desire to see God, insofar, as this importance is put into the context of a sinful world. . . .
>
> The history of prehistoric man inhabiting this earth thousands of centuries ago is a closed book to us; but in connection with what has been said about the influence which the community asserts over the individual, it is possible to see mankind in its totality as the cause of the present state of affairs. Sin has taken root in the human community, in order to rule over it as a tyrannizing power. Whoever is born into this community is irrevocably delivered to this power.[5]

SIN OF THE WORLD

Too long theologians and biblical exegetes emphasized Adam's individual sin that had set us up in a weakened condition to commit our own individual sins. Today theologians are accentuating the communal aspect of original sin and mankind's solidarity as a community in wrongdoing. Although we still retain our free will not to sin, modern thinkers stress how our freedom is affected by forces around us, stemming from societal influences that collectively have been mounting in a favoring of self-centeredness since the sin of the first man.

St. John calls this collective solidarity in sinfulness the "sin of the world" (*hamartia* in Greek). This is the brokenness of the whole world and goes far beyond the mere totaling of all individual sins. It refers to the sin of mankind as a united community in sinfulness.

St. Paul dramatically describes Christ's entrance into this human sinfulness. "For our sake God made the sinless one into sin, so that in him we might become the goodness of God" (2 C 5:21). Jesus, by consenting to be born into the human family, inserts Himself into our broken, human history. He bears the burden of all of us as we all are united in sin. Yet St. John the Baptist exclaimed: "Look, there is the lamb of God that takes away the sin of the world" (Jn 1:29).

Jesus came into our world and still enters into our lives to bear our sins. He subjected Himself in His temptations, as we discussed earlier, to the human brokenness in the communal solidarity to choose between obedience to God or self-centeredness. By overcoming His temptations, He broke the power of the "sin of the world." But more, He became the one to set us captives free (Lk 4:18). He is able after His death and resurrection to release His Spirit into the world to fashion a new creation, a solidarity of like-minded persons who "live by the truth and in love" (Ep 4:15). It is His Spirit that fashions the new creation into a one Body, the Church, of whose Head is Jesus Christ (Ep 4:16).

WHOLENESS AND BROKENNESS

C hrist is the Head and He is the Healer, the one who alone can bring the human race into a wholeness, a unity of loving persons living for each other and carrying each other's troubles (Gal 6:2). Yet our world is truly still broken and fragmented. We live in the hope of being freed from the sinful "slavery to decadence" (Rm 8:21) that forces us and the whole material world to groan in travail.

There has been so much evident brokenness in the past history of our human ancestors. The tower of Babel is a myth that well describes human beings who sought to reach God's level of being by their own powers with the universal alienation resulting that man no longer could communicate with God or fellow-man by the universal language of love.

A "spiritual army of evil" (Ep 6:12) enforces darkness upon all mankind in all generations. This accumulated brokenness shows itself in our own existential situation in which we presently live. We are being sucked down into its dark pits continuously in our families, in our culture, in our economic and political arenas, in our churches even. Like a poisonous gas that infiltrates every molecule of air that we breathe, we breathe in sin and selfishness in our every waking moment. The law, of the unredeemed jungle is all about us exerting its tyrannical power over us. This same law, enforced by the "lord of the flies," is within us, beating us slaves into a quivering submission.

COLLECTIVE GUILT

One of the greatest forces of evil in our modern, broken world stems from collectivization. As the family and clan developed into a village, a town, a city, a state, a country, a nation and allied countries, the individual yielded his moral decisions to the impersonalized group. Groups are not primarily organized for evil, but gradually there usually results a tendency toward what Professor Irving Janis of Yale University coins as "group-think."[6]

Such "sinfulness" shows itself in the group as a whole, feeling infallible. Any action it unanimously agrees on is automatically considered as good. Evil can be done by individuals, so group-think thinks, and not by the group. The group always looks out for the greatest good. In such thinking the enemy that thinks differently from the group is basically evil. Fighting such an enemy is to help God in enforcing righteousness.

This thinking drove Jesus to the cross. Such rationalization allowed white men to kill 100,000 Indians in California alone between 1820 and 1850. God on the side of the white men, "in whom there is no darkness," developed the slave trade in which thousands of defenseless blacks from the African villages were herded as brute animals into the holes of ships, chained in their excretions, and then sold to farmers, "genteel" folk, politicians, priests and nuns to be their indentured slaves.

We were always as an American nation doing good and never evil in all of our wars, especially in My Lai of Vietnam, or in our political tactics of government, of CIA operations or Watergate. We bombed Hiroshima and Nagasaki because God gave us the atom bomb to keep America safe from the Japs. The American Indians had no right to their lands because the white men were moving westward and needed their hunting grounds and forests to build factories and bring about a higher standard of living for white men.

Hitler could whip a nation of Christians into immobility as he ordered six million Jews and other "undesirables" to be gassed in chambers. Turks could wipe out a million and a half Armenians and in our own days nearly a million in Cambodia have seen death. Still no one seems very perturbed! Millions have been dying of starvation in the sub-Sahara and we as a group hear it once and then get on with earning more money for our rich nation.

One of our greatest industries is supplying bombers, bombs, tanks, submarines and anything else that will kill and destroy efficiently to any nation, even to two nations in deadly combat who destroy themselves with our armaments, while we become "fatter" by their hateful holocausts.

But perhaps our duplicity is most seen in great American corporations entering undeveloped countries to bring them "salvation" by setting up factories and plants to exhaust the resources of such countries in huge dividends that end up in the pocket of the few stockholders back home. Our gross imposition of American "culture" upon wholesome, simple peoples has turned millions in Africa, South America and Asia into materialists seeking more and more sense pleasures while losing their former transcendent values.

COLLECTIVE, CULTIC SINFULNESS

Religion was meant to be the force in society that would fight for individual rights and the uniqueness of each person in freedom to develop fully in a human society of peace and harmony. But what sins have collectively been perpetrated by organized religions over the centuries! What hatred and violent persecutions Christians in the name of their meek Lamb of God have inflicted upon the Jewish people! In the name of God colonialists marched hand in hand with the missionary priests into South, Central and North America to "Christianize" the natives and bring them out of darkness into the light of Christ.

Colonialists from "Christian" countries of Spain, Portugal, France, England and Holland poured into Africa to save the blacks from their pagan idols by telling them of the good, bourgeois God that they adored. Afrikaners in the name of their Dutch Reformed Church insist that *apartheid* is a part of true Christianity because God predestines some white men to enjoy the wealth of the earth while other blacks and non-whites are reduced to chattel.

In our collective brokenness who can ever adequately describe the absurdity of Christians in "just," even "religious" wars, killing other Christians and non-Christians over the 2,000 years of Christianity's existence? Who can describe the worldliness in Church leaders in past history, of popes, cardinals, bishops and priests? What charges of simony, magic, superstition, guilts and fears cultic leaders imposed upon the "faithful!"

FROM DARKNESS TO LIGHT

W ho of us have not experienced, even daily, as we watch the evening news coverage from all over the world enter into our living rooms via television, a sense of mounting fear before so much brokenness and alienation within the human race, so much increasing violence, killings, crimes committed on all levels of human life? We are left breathless and in perplexed wonderment at where our world is going? Fears and anxieties load our unconscious with guilt and remorse that we do not understand. Above all, we no longer can get on top of these cataclysmic problems and see a hopeful solution in a better President, a more upright Congress or in new committees or better laws.

The proportions of our modern problems increase as the confidence in our own human powers to create a better world diminishes until we seem totally powerless to do anything but to insulate ourselves from the menacing problems by distractions. To add to the brokenness in the world some of us turn to a religion that comforts and promises a Heaven awaiting us if we only do not become too preoccupied with the "world."

Others distract themselves by alcohol, drugs, travel, fast cars or sailboats, sports, music, art or by earning more money in order to buy the "good" things of this life. All such distractions, when they move us toward self-centeredness, only add to the darkness in the world.

The collectivity cannot solve its own problems. It has no personalized consciousness. It lacks the ability to claim the guilt and repair the damage by virtuous living. For it is only made up of individuals, you and me. We must return to hear again the call of the Prophets of old to return to God in a communal and individual conversion. It is a rending of our hearts, not sacrifices or holocausts, that God wants from us.

The Prophet Isaiah gives us the light that can lead us out of our collective darkness:

> A sinful nation, a people weighed down with guilt,
> a breed of wrong-doers, perverted sons.
> They have abandoned Yahweh, despised the Holy One of Israel,
> they have turned away from him.
>
> . . . 'Come now, let us talk this over,'
> says Yahweh.
> 'Though your sins are like scarlet,
> they shall be as white as snow;
> though they are red as crimson,
> they shall be like wool.
>
> If you are willing to obey,
> you shall eat the good things of the earth.
> But if you persist in rebellion,
> the sword shall eat you instead.'
> The mouth of Yahweh has spoken (Is 1:4-20).

The Prophet Jeremiah still asks the question of us moderns today: "Have you not brought this on yourself, by abandoning Yahweh your God?" (Jr 2:16-17).

CHRIST, THE WAY

J esus, God-Man, has taken the world's brokenness upon Himself that He might overthrow it and create a new world. He defeats sin and death, meaninglessness and corruption in this world by pouring out His Holy Spirit upon us. This Spirit of love drives us into the desert of our inner darkness and sinfulness. He will convince us of sin. He will lead us to all truth but first He will lead us to true repentance.

> And when he comes,
> he will show the world how wrong it was,
> about sin,
> and about who was in the right,
> and about judgment:
> about sin:
> proved by their refusal to believe in me;
> about who was in the right:
> proved by my going to the Father
> and your seeing me no more;
> about judgment:
> proved by the prince of this world being already condemned.
> (Jn 16:8-11)

He alone can uproot selfishness in the world by uprooting it from our hearts. He does this by pouring the love of God into our hearts (Rm 5:5). In this personalized love of our Heavenly Father, manifested in Jesus always dying for you and me (Gal 2:20), we can burst forth from the tentacles of selfishness into the true freedom of children of God. This Spirit fashions us, once our solidarity in sin with a groaning world has been broken up, into a new oneness in the Body of Christ. "There is one Body, one Spirit, just as you were all called into one and the same hope when you were called. There is one Lord, one faith, one baptism, and one God who is Father of all, over all through all and within all" (Ep 4:4-6).

VICTORY OVER SIN

T hrough His Resurrection, Jesus is able to touch us in our confining fears and petty slaveries and lead us out into true freedom. It is His

Spirit, who alone can lead us "to know Christ and the power of His resurrection and to share His sufferings by reproducing the pattern of His death. That is the way I can hope to take my place in the resurrection of the dead" (Ph 3:10-12). We are as free as we desire to surrender to the Spirit of Jesus to take away all our fears and even now to live in the freeing power of the Risen Lord. With St. Paul, we can boast of our own weakness (2 C 11:30) for our total strength is in Jesus Christ. ". . . and by God's doing He has become our wisdom, and our virtue, and our holiness and our freedom" (1 C 1:30). We are free because "we are those who have the mind of Christ" (1 C 2:16).

The Risen Jesus has conquered in our lives by the revelation of His Spirit. We are becoming freed from sin and death and the false values, "the sin of the world" and can live in the freedom of the risen people of God as we refuse to live in the solidarity of sinful people who have been called by God "to be holy and spotless, and to live through love in his presence" (Ep 1:4).

Jesus has conquered death and He conquers our hearts as we allow Him to be Lord in our lives. True freedom from sinful brokenness is the progressive surrender in love to Him so that in each moment He is Lord of the universe. He is the inner force that allows us to catch this moment of history with all its brokenness, filth, confining meaning-lessness and raise it unto the level of God's eternal now. His Spirit brings us into an ever-growing awareness of our true dignity before the world. In that dignity of being loved infinitely by God in Christ Jesus, we are free to love as He loves us. Freedom, as God gives us this great gift, is nothing less than the gift of loving ourselves and the entire world as God loves us and with God's love in us.

SOLIDARITY IN THE BODY OF CHRIST

Our conversion each moment is a series of saying "yes" to the dictates of Jesus' Spirit of love and "no" to the sin of the world. When we act in this "yes" of love, we become "reconcilers." God gave us this work in Jesus Christ of handing on this reconciliation (2 C 5:18). We have the dignity by our service within the Body of Christ to fight the darkness and sinfulness in the world and to reconcile it through Christ back to the Father.

Jesus is not only the Alpha (Jn 1:2), but He is now, through His members in His Body, the Church, inserted into the cosmos and is bringing the material world to its fullness. He continues to be the Healer to the broken ones of this world. He is bringing the material world to its fullness. He is also the Omega, the goal, the end towards which every creature is being drawn as by a magnetic force of personal love.

The evil of the world in its solidarity of brokenness is conquered and transformed into goodness and wholeness by Christ in His members. Jesus is now present and is now effecting the victory over the dark powers of cosmic evil. Yet He will come in glory in the *Parousia*, when the Gospel of Jesus will have been preached to the entire universe. Our hope is an active hope that testifies as we work against negative elements of selfishness in the world that Christian redemption embraces also the materiality of the whole cosmos that now is so united in its groaning travail. The Good News that our broken world must hear is that Jesus Christ is already here in this dark world and is bringing about the Kingdom of Heaven in our lives and through us in the whole world. In an exciting way we Christians must spread the good news that we have already experienced within ourselves and within our Christian communities that God is now communicating Himself to us in our darkness by the bright light of His fully realized Word—Jesus Christ. Into the dark silence of our inner world of brokenness the brightness of Jesus enters and brings eternal healing and everlasting life.

MEDITATION ON A BROKEN WORLD

In the end, man destroyed the heaven that was called earth.

The earth had been beautiful until the spirit of man moved over it and destroyed all things.

And man said . . .

Let there be darkness . . . and there was darkness.

And man liked the darkness; so he called the darkness "security;"

And he divided himself into races and religions and classes of society.

And there was no evening and no morning on the seventh day before the end.

And man said . . .

Let there be a strong government to control us in our darkness.

Let there be armies to control our bodies, so that we may learn to kill
      one another neatly and efficiently in our darkness.

And there was no evening and no morning on the sixth day before the
      end.

And man said . . .

Let there be rockets and bombs to kill faster and easier;

Let there be gas chambers and furnaces to be more thorough.

And there was no evening and no morning on the fifth day before the
      end.

And man said . . .

Let there be drugs and other forms of escape, for there is this constant
annoyance—REALITY which is disturbing our comfort.

And there was no morning and no evening on the fourth day before the
      end.

And man said . . .

Let there be division among the nations, so that we may know who is
      our common enemy.

And there was no morning and no evening on the third day before the
      end.

And finally man said . . .

Let us create God in our image.

Let some other god compete with us.

Let us say that God thinks—as we think.

                hates—as we hate.

                and kills—as we kill.

And there was no morning and no evening on the second day before
      the end.

On the LAST day there was a great noise on the face of the earth.

Fire consumed the beautiful globe, and there was———SILENCE.

The blackened earth now rested to worship the one true God;

And God saw all that man had done

           and in the silence over the smoldering ruins

           HE WEPT.

CHAPTER SEVEN

A BROKEN CHURCH

T he American artist, William Zdinak, has painted a dramatic
picture that he has called, "In His Image." He has portrayed the
face of Jesus, crowned with thorns and hanging on the cross. But what
is striking about this painting is that he has carefully and clearly
painted the faces of "real" human beings into the face and the body of
Christ. These are not only famous personages like Pope Paul VI, J.F.
Kennedy and Martin Luther King Jr., but also depicted, fashioning the
suffering, broken body of Christ, are not so famous persons, ordinary
persons. The message of the artist is a profound one. The whole
human race, every human person, has been made according to His
image (Gn 1:26). All of us, men and women from the first beginning
of the human race until the last person to exist on the earth, have been
called to fashion the body of Jesus Christ. But this "building-up" of
Christ's body, the Church, is being accomplished at all times through
the broken sufferings of its members, as we fill up the sufferings of
Christ's body, the Church (Col 1:24).

IDEAS OF CHURCH

M uch of the brokenness found within the Church comes from the
various ways in which down through the centuries Christians
have conceived the Church to be. For some Christians the word
church refers only to a physical building, a place where they go to do
certain things. They go to church to say prayers, to hear sermons, to
"go to Mass" on Sundays, to meet other friends in order to socialize.
It can be a place for some Christians to have their problems solved and
to obtain "graces" and strength to cope with life's pressures.

For other Christians, especially Roman Catholics and Orthodox, both for those who make up the clergy and for the laity, long brain-washed by a paternalistic authority, the Church is priests and bishops and popes. This is usually at the basis of such remarks as, "The Church teaches" or "The Church ought to do something about that problem."

A more adequate understanding of *church* can come only if we go back to Holy Scripture and see the Church in the light of God's salvific plan for the whole world. In Greek, Church is *ekklesia*, the commu-nity of those "called out" to become God's chosen people. In the Old Testament we see the primitive Church as the *Qahal*, the Lord's assembly that He calls together into a loving covenant with Himself as its center of worship and adoring living. The People of God, called Israel, were brought together by God's gratuitous election (Dt 7:7).

The New Testament Church is the People of God that belong to Jesus. St. Paul writes that they "form the Israel of God" (Ga 6:16). They are "the holy people of Jesus Christ" (1 C 1:2). Jesus brought His Church into being by His blood (Ac 20:28). Thus Christians are those who live by the power of the death and resurrection of Jesus. Jesus pours out His Spirit, who frees Christians from sin and death, from self-centeredness, and forms them into a one body that has Jesus Risen as its head (Ep 4:4; Col 1:18).

A NEW TEMPLE

The temple of the Old Testament was the resting place for the Ark of the Covenant. God "pitched His tent" among His chosen People. That "tent of the meeting" and the temple of Jerusalem were the place where the holy God of Israel met His sinful people and developed that love relationship.

But when God's Word became incarnate and literally took up His abode among the human race that sat in darkness (Jn 1:14), Jesus Christ became the new temple, the final place where God and sinful mankind would meet and be reconciled. Jesus claimed that He now was the temple of God, the New Jerusalem, and when He would be destroyed by death, He would raise up His body, the everlasting temple, to new glory (Jn 2:19, 21-22).

In a wonderful manner by the release of His Holy Spirit within His followers, Jesus forms us Christians into the temple of the Holy Spirit.

> Didn't you realize that you were God's temple and that the Spirit of God was living among you? If anybody should destroy the temple of God, God will destroy him, because the temple of God is sacred; and you are that temple (1 C 3:16-17).

Pentecost, as a continued event, brings us into a one Body, the Church, since Christ is the Head and we belong to Him as His members. In that same Spirit we are to be empowered to proclaim the mystery of God's plan of salvation to the whole world. We are to love one another in the fellowship (*koinonia*) or communion of the Holy Spirit who pours the love of God into our hearts (Rm 5:5). In that love for one another we are to be of humble service (*diakonia*) to all human beings as to our own brothers and sisters.

The Church is to live by this great, mysterious reality. God "has put all things under his feet, and made him, as the ruler of everything, the head of the Church; which is his body, the fullness of him who fills the whole creation" (Ep 1:22-23).

THE BODY OF CHRIST

St. Paul met Jesus in vision on the road to Damascus (Ac 9:4) and learned a lesson about Church that he never forgot. Persecuting the followers of Jesus, Paul was really persecuting Jesus. He would develop in his preaching and writing an ecclesiology that would present the Church, the People who belong to Jesus, as the very Body of the total Jesus Christ risen. A new man is created, the whole Christ, as individuals live in Him. It is not a group of persons assembled together to remember the historical Jesus. Jesus has more than an extrinsic influence upon His true followers.

They are to put on Christ "All of you are one in Christ Jesus" (Gal 3:28). F.X. Durrwell, the Pauline scholar, insists that the Christian forms a *real* oneness with Jesus "by a change transforming him into one man, one body" (Ep 2:15-16) into the bodily Christ.[1] The risen Savior lives within the Christian in a unique union that forms not only a true body between Christ and the individual but between Christ and all His members who live in Him.

TENSIONED UNION

T his sublime doctrine of the Church as found in the New Testament writings, that describes in the words of St. Cyprian the Church as "a people brought into unity from the unity of the Father, the Son and the Holy Spirit,"[2] alas, has not always been so ideally lived out in the history of the Church. Even St. Paul realized the tension between what the Church should be and what it actually was in his times. The Church is the new and holy temple of Jerusalem, made one and spotless by the Spirit of love. Yet St. Paul had to rebuke the Christians at Corinth for immorality and dissension, factions and quarrels, ignorance and pride.

The Church is holy and yet it is made up of sinful men and women. It is partially divine by God's gifts of the sacraments and the preached Word; yet it is human and very material. It is to have no part of the world's thinking yet it would necessarily be in the world as a leaven. As the Bride of Christ, the Church shares in His power and holiness. Yet the Church also is the prostitute needing conversion and reform. It shares in Christ's shepherding of the lost, but it also is the lost sheep that always needs finding.

The Church possesses the fullness of the risen Jesus in having received from Him all that is necessary to bring the world into holiness without any error or power from the "gates of Hell." Yet as individuals we can lose this great treasure or render it ineffective and thus the Church can become sinful and fall into error.

The Church, like the personhood of Jesus Christ, admits of a divine and a human element. It possesses the Voice by which the people of Christ can be called together in His name and be divinized by the divine power of the Church. It can also be seen as the Church that answers that Voice and in this aspect we can usually discern much that is not only human and material in the Church, but even broken, worldly and sinful.[3] It is divine insofar as its power to lead all men and women into a sharing community whose origin is found in the Trinity. But it is without any separation yet distinctly made up of human, frail beings who are not yet fully what they should be.

AN OVERLY SPIRITUAL CHURCH

V atican II's Dogmatic Constitution on the Church in the Modern World stresses more than any other previous church documents that the Church is a Pilgrim-Church. It is in need of the sacraments, especially Baptism, Reconciliation and the Eucharist, in order to be alive in Christ and fulfill its divine mission to bring salvation to the world.

What evils have been brought about, especially by omission, when the Church in its earthly pilrimage forgot its precarious, fragile possession of holiness and Jesus' Spirit and acted only as a "spiritual" Church, ignoring its human aspect! In such thinking it is an already, once and for all holy Church. There can be no defects, no errors, no need for repentance; in a word, no need for the saving power of God. This is seen in the broken history of Christianity in the many sects that broke away in holy pride from the struggling human, visible Church to settle down in splendid isolation from a sinful world because the Church is a saved group of self-congratulating saved members.

This ultra-supernaturalistic Church ultimately denies the Incarnation and God's love for His material world and His active presence through His true Church in that broken world. It denies that God is a concerned God that pursues His people, that continually forgives and re-establishes His merciful covenant with His sinful people. Ultimately such a distorted view of the Church stems from a spiritual pride and lack of faith and hope in God to bring about a new creation out of the erring mass of humanity.

To believe that the Church is holy, even when one can see only brokenness in its tired, desert pilgrims, requires hope that such holiness is not intrinsic to the Church but only in Jesus Christ. The Church is to become holy as it unites its ministry to the power of Jesus' Spirit.

> For we must be content to hope that we shall be saved—
> our salvation is not in sight, we should not have to be
> hoping for it if it were—but, as I say, we must hope to be
> saved since we are not saved yet—it is something we must
> wait for with patience (Rm 8:24-25).

A WORLDLY CHURCH

But perhaps the greatest scandals and brokenness have come to the world when members of the Church, both its leaders in authority and its individual members, have forgotten the spiritual power given to it to serve a broken world. Such a Church through its members settles down either to worldly complacency, forgetting its need for discipline and humble vigilance, or to a compromise with the "world, the flesh and the devil." Such a Church in the desert either wants to return to the flesh pots of slavery in Egypt or to erect in the desert its golden calf. It is a Church that is neither hot nor cold but tepid (Rv 3:15-16). It forgets what St. Peter warns the early Church: "The time has come for the judgment to begin at the household of God" (1 P 4:17).

The Christian Church kept alive the mystery of the God-man, both divine and human, and its own *theandric*, divine-human makeup, during its first few centuries of existence. Its members lived the mystery of Christ's death and resurrection as they were constantly faced with physical martyrdom. But when it allowed Constantine and his many political successors to manipulate the Church away from its "suffering-servant" role, then the Church became all too worldly and all too broken.

Alfred Whitehead, the noted philosopher, writes:

> When the Western world accepted Christianity, Caesar conquered . . . The brief Galilean vision of humility flickered throughout the ages, uncertainly. In the official formulation of religion, it has assumed the trivial form of the mere attribution to Jews that they cherished a misconception about their Messias. But their deeper idolatory of fashioning of God in the image of the Egyptian, Persian and Roman imperial rulers was retained. The Church gave unto God the attributes which belonged exclusively to Caesar.[4]

The awesome freedom, that Jesus challenged His followers to live by that came only through death to self-love and a resurrection in humble, loving service, was often forgotten, both in Eastern and Western forms of Christianity. In the words of Dostoievsky in his novel, *The Brothers Karamazov*, the sheep begged the shepherds to give them a religion of miracles, mystery and authority. What was originally conceived of as a *symphonia*, a harmony of mutual cooperation between emperors in Constantinople and in Moscow and Eastern Church leaders all too often let to a sycophant hierarchy that compromised the Gospel values for political and religious power and riches.

THE SOVEREIGN POPE

In the West, amidst invasions by barbarians and persecutions by so-called Christian princes, the Church leaders developed the sovereign rights for papal authority even over kings of this world. Under such "reforming" Popes as Gregory VII, Innocent III and Boniface VIII the Church became synonomous with clerics: priests, bishops and popes. The Pope of Rome becomes the Vicar of Christ. He wields a double sword, church and civil authority, with no limitation but what God has given him in the "plenipotentiary" power to do all to bring the world to Christ.

But all too often the Gospel values were forgotten as canon law replaced the Good News of Jesus. At the end of the 11th century under the Gregorian reforms of Pope Gregory VII (†1085), prepared by the absolutizing of the powers of the Pope under Popes Leo IX and Nicholas II, the Papacy's chief concern was to assert its rights over all secular power as well as all Eastern and Western bishops. Pope Gregory VII's statement[5] illustrates how far the "Church" had wandered from the crucified Christ: "The Church is not a servant, but a *mistress (Domina)*."

Along with such a concept of Church as a Ruler, the concept of the Pope as a reigning sovereign evolved. Privileges and insignia surrounded the Pope and bishops that they copied from ruling princes and kings. Pomp, processions, places for residences and cathedrals adorned with marble and gold replaced the humble surroundings of the Upper Room where the Master of all washed the feet of His disciples. St. Bernard complained to his former subject, Pope Eugenius III (†1153): "When the pope, clad in silk, covered with gold and jewels, rides out on his white horse, escorted by soldiers and servants, he looks more like Constantine's successor than St. Peter's."[6]

All of us, who have seen modern Popes carried aloft on the *sedes gestatoria* through cheering crowds, have wondered also whether the true power that Jesus gave to Peter and His disciples to rival each other in humble service has not been replaced by a cheap imitation of the power of the world.

HERESY IN THE CHURCH

W ho can ever measure the degree of brokenness and evils that heresies brought to the Church of Christ? Jesus had promised His disciples that His Spirit would reveal to them all they needed to know about Himself and truth. Yet from even the earliest times we see brokenness brought into the Body of Christ through false teachers. St. Paul continually warned the early Christians about such false teachers.

At first such heresies attacked the mystery of the nature of Jesus Christ and hence the fundamental doctrine of the Christian faith about the Trinity. Arianism taught that Jesus was merely a man adopted by God as His Son. For centuries this heresy rocked the Christian Churches in the East and West. The Spirit moved the bishops to come together in ecumenical Councils, especially the first two, Nicaea (325) and Constantinople I (381), and to define in dogmatic terms that Jesus was "*homoousios*," of the same nature as the Father.

St. Hilary of Poitiers, a Father of the Latin Church, wrote in the fourth century:

> The guilt of the heretics and blasphemers compels us to undertake what is unlawful, to scale arduous heights, to speak of the ineffable and to trespass upon forbidden places . . . we are forced to raise our lowly words to subjects which cannot be described. By the guilt of another we are forced into guilt, so that what should have been restricted to the pious contemplation of our minds is now exposed to the dangers of human speech.[7]

Other heresies concerning the nature of Christ such as Nestorianism and Monophysitism split the Church into three parts: the Roman and Byzantine Churches strenuously adhered to the orthodox teachings about Christ as defined in the Councils of Ephesus (431) and Chalcedon (451) while the Assyrian Church and those of Syria,

Armenia, Egypt and Ethiopia broke the unity in the Body of Christ. For over fifteen centuries these church-bodies have existed without any true sharing with their fellow Christians. This is brokenness! And yet how much of such separation must be laid at the door of politics and nationalism, a repeated root cause throughout the following centuries for breaking up of the Body of Christ.

In the West heresies of Montanism, Donatism and Pelagianism added their own brokenness and alienation within Western Christianity. The list of heresies would fill volumes but they all have one common effect. The unity in the Church is attacked and a position false to the true teaching as found in Holy Scripture and the traditional teaching authority of the Church is obstinately maintained. Rival Churches, possessing "bits of gold," split off and the whole Body of Christ becomes weakened.

SCHISMS

Some of the greatest evils in the Church have resulted, not from gross heresies spewed out in ignorance, but from suspicions and intolerance between Christian Churches. This element of brokenness is poignantly seen in the great splits that occurred between the Roman and Byzantine Churches in the 11th to the 13th centuries and the Roman and Protestant Churches of the 16th century.

Both Eastern and Western Churches have suffered greatly due to the separation from each other. This alienation and estrangement developed gradually and no one side or no one person is more guilty for such a tragedy than any other. Both the Roman and Byzantine churchmen, from the time of Patriarch Photius in the ninth century, to Cardinal Humberto in 1054, with the mutual exommunications hurled at each, to the Crusades, especially the 4th Crusade of 1204 under the blessing of Pope Innocent III, to the disastrous attempts at reunion in the Councils of Lyons II (1279) and Florence (1439) added to a spirit of triumphalism. This spirit entrenched itself into a fixed and haughty position of being the sole carrier of true Christian traditions as opposed to the errors of the Latins or Greeks.

Suspicions hardened into hatred as both sides refused to pray together. More brokenness fell upon the Eastern Churches in the double form of phyletism and the Islamic conquests. Phyletism de manded that each Eastern nation should be granted its own national church which fragmented the Eastern Christian ethos into Churches that lost true sharing with each other, but, more disastrously, such Churches all too often became puppets for national politics, as we see in present day U.S.S.R. and the other Slavic countries.

Martin Luther was a zealous reformer who wanted nothing but the renewal of true Christianity in the Roman Church. His objections echoed a real need for an inner reformation of the Western Church. But he was not heard as Roman officials pushed him to a complete break. With the backing of powerful German princes, he found himself as head of a new Church. Here too was the the beginning of other churches founded by John Calvin, Ulrich Zwingli, Henry VIII, John Knox and a host of others down to our modern times.

Who can tell of the agony and religious wars fought in families, countries and throughout the world, all in the name of Christianity? What brokenness as such church bodies harden themselves in polemical, doctrinal positions and refuse to change or be mutually aided by each other? Denominations become more important than the one Christian faith. History becomes more powerful than the presence of our Lord. Human traditions and man-made theologies replace the Gospel and Christ's light. Church structures push out the Spirit of true life. Our own wall and barriers keep out Divine Love. Our "positions" must be maintained over Divine Truth; our worldly power over our brotherhood in Jesus. Our "Church" opposes your "Church" and the community of God's family is forgotten.

PHILOSOPHY VERSUS THE GOSPEL

No religion is passed on except through the vehicle of a formulated philosophy. The early thinkers in Christianity, beginning with St. Justin the Martyr in the 2nd century, St. Irenaeus, Clement and Origen of Alexandria, down through the numerous writings of St. Augustine, St. Thomas Aquinas, the Scholastic writers, the Protestant Reformers, down to Teilhard de Chardin, all used the philosophical constructs of their age. What thinker could ever unravel the skein of brokenness and evil brought into the Christian Churches through Gnostic and Platonic dualism? Such a backdrop that tainted the true message of the Gospel of Jesus pitted God as Spirit against an evil, material world. Virginity was superior to marriage and monasticism would be the ideal form for sincere Christians eager to "save their souls."

In such a framework man, being made up of matter, is basically corrupt and can do no good. Grace becomes an extrinsic thing that God trades with us for works done in patient suffering. The less any Christian can have to do with the material world the better a Christian he or she will be. A very self-centered piety develops in a vertical relation between God and myself, while my social relationships with other human beings have little to do with Christianity.

The separation of the sacred and the secular, of contemplation and action, of body and soul, nature and supernature is found in nearly all Christian Churches.

Not only much unnecessary sufferings have been introduced into Christianity through the exaltation of philosophy over the Gospel but the greatest tragedy has resulted in rendering Christianity as an innocuous force to direct our universe into enriching fulfillment. When church leaders canonize religious teachings, more rooted in philosophy than in God's living Word, we see so often a Christianity that is static, legalistic, impersonal and other-worldly. Such a religious approach creates its own type of God and minor idols that make Christianity not a vital force and leaven in the world but a dehumanizing factor that opposes what true religion is meant to accomplish.

How often we have seen this in certain Churches fostering racism as in the Dutch Reformed Church of South Africa and its apartheid policy, based on a sinful interpretation of Christianity. Millions of German Christians were muted into silence as Hitler put to death six million people who did not measure up to his concept of a super race. A pope is seen blessing Italian tanks before launching an invasion of Ethiopia. Millions of Catholics suffer in the brokenness of divorce and remarriage while chancery officials and Vatican curialists hurl excommunications at them. What do most churchmen have to say to the suffering homosexuals about the healing love of Jesus?

While most Christian Churches are busy running raffles and

bingo, inner cities are being overrun by rats and vermin, crime and gutted out buildings. Failure to speak out on war, women's rights, racism, nuclear arms, the population explosion has rendered Christianity an anemic force in our modern world. Preachers and theologians find comfort in preaching a Christianity that does not rock the established order. And all too often when they do, inquisitional tactics and trials are resorted to in order to suppress such free exploration into new areas of knowledge and possibilities.

A CRY FOR A SAVIOR

T o continue to list the factors in the Body of Christ that add to its brokenness would be endless and of no greater avail. All around us Christians we are confronted with evil in our Church where we would expect only good. Bitter and disillusioned, we could easily turn away and slink off into isolated loneliness. But where can we go? We belong to Christ. He is our Head. He is the fullness of life. Just as He told His bitter and disillusioned disciples at Emmaus, so He tells us today:

> You foolish men! So slow to believe the full message of the prophets! Was it not ordained that the Christ should suffer and so enter into his glory? (Lk 24:25-26).

When we can, as a corporate Church, the Body of Christ, realize our awful broken condition and our complete incapacity to be our own healer, then we can cry out in earnest. "Come, Lord Jesus. Marana tha!" Then we can learn to live in the brokenness of the first disciples of Jesus who betrayed Him and ran away from their crucified Savior. Like them, we can hope that the risen Jesus will continue to release His Spirit into all of us His members and transform little by little the harlot-wife of Hosea into the faithful Bride of Christ.

MEDITATION

A BROKEN CHURCH

God called His people
to be his chosen friends.
"If Yahweh set His heart

on you and chose you,
it was not because you
outnumbered other peoples.
You were the least of all peoples.
It was for love of you
that I brought you out of Egypt
and freed you from slavery.

And this alone I asked of you,
that you would keep My commandments
and love one another
as I have loved you.
I promised that you would increase.
I would bless your offspring
and the work of your hands.

But My people has forgotten Me.
They have exchanged My glory
for the darkness of their own idols.
They have abandoned Me, Yahweh,
the Fountain of living water,
only to dig cisterns for themselves
that hold no water.

I sent in due time
My Son to dwell among them.
He came as a light
but the darkness in their hearts
rose up in mock righteousness
and snuffed out the Light of the world.
Yet I glorified Him
and raised Him to new power.
He poured out His Spirit
to breathe My breath of life
into the dry bones of the remnant
of My broken people.

And they rose with Him
to form a part of His Body.
They were the "called-out" assembly,

belonging to Him as the branches
belong to the vine.
He gave them power
to heal the sick and broken,
to give Himself as the Bread of life
to the starving of the world.

They preached the Good News
that He and I are one
and in our Spirit of love
We wanted to make our abode
within them as in a new temple.
They baptized in our triune family,
Father, Son and Spirit.
They brought the saving Word
to nations unto the ends of the world.

I betrothed that people to My Son
as a Bride to the Bridegroom.
That bride was virginal and comely,
thrilling the heart of her Spouse.
And yet how she grew restless,
desirous of new riches and power.
She traded His glory
for the tinsel of this world.
She harloted herself
to the princes of this world.

Broken and betrayed, she weeps
in the desert to return to her Spouse.
'I will rise and go back
to my first and true Husband.
I will confess my sins.
I will weep for forgiveness
and He will answer my cry.'

My Son will take her back.
He will lure her to Himself
and heal her of her brokenness.
He will bring her into new health

with tenderness and love.
And out of her will come
a new progeny of children
more numerous than the stars above
and the grains of sand on the seashore.

This is what My Son will do
if you, My People,
will claim Me as your God
and My Son as your Spouse.''

CHAPTER EIGHT

I AM BROKEN

There is not one who reads these words who cannot claim his or her share of brokenness. This shows itself at various times of our lives in varying degrees of intensity. We can all see the progressive degrees of physical brokenness as we move each day a bit closer to that final earthly moment of total dissolution from our material existence.

But what brokenness do we find in our psychic order! What fears assail us with unceasing cruelty day and night! Doubts, anger, depression, hatred and unforgiveness seethe within us as a gigantic, smoldering volcano that needs the slightest tremor to pour forth its molten lava in cruel actions, biting words or fitful retreat into lonely solitude.

Then there are the terrifying dark nights of the spiritual world. We cry out to see again the face of God. Yet there is only darkness! Not only does God seem to be absent, but we seem to have lost all faith in Him. What blasphemous thoughts possess us! Down deeper we go into my life? How do I know God really exists? Is Jesus anything but a man in history? Darkness rolls upon darkness like belching clouds of blackness racing to cover each other with its own ugliness.

In all of this we cringe in our brokenness, hoping, begging, searching for a way out of such absurdity and utter meaninglessness. When will it all end? There is so much of it and we become so tired of it!

THE DAIMONIC

The ancient Greeks referred to the *daemon* or *daimon* within all of us. This refers both to the light and the darkness inside of us. We have both positive and negative elements stored up in giant propor tions to be actualized in creative or destructive deeds. We all veer dizzily, now toward madness, at times, noble love or toward cruel selfishness.

The great German poet, Rainer Maria Rilke (†1926), expressed the two faces of the same coin when he wrote: "If my devils are to leave me, I am afraid my angels will take flight as well."[1]

The daimonic in all of us can be unto good or evil; often it is a bit of both. It is never totally oriented toward beauty and creativity. Nor is it completely aimed at the ugly and the destructive. We posses much brokenness within ourselves. But in that very brokenness lies unsuspected richness in new love energy.

We can perhaps understand this relationship by going to the root meaning of *devil* and *symbol*. *Diabolos* in Greek literally means to tear apart (*dia-bollein*). The opposite of diabolic is symbolic which is derived from the Greek verb *sym-bollein*, to throw together or to unite. Dr. Rollo May, the popular, American author and psychoanalyst, gives us a keen insight, in his explanation of the daimonic:

> There lie in these words tremendous implications with respect to an ontology of good and evil. The *symbolic* is that which draws together, ties, integrates the individual in himself and with his group; the *diabolic*, in contrast, is that which disintegrates and tears apart. Both of these are present in the daimonic.[2]

INTERMESHED IN HUMANITY

We have seen already both from Holy Scripture and human history how we form a solidarity with the whole world in our brokenness, in "the sin of the world." We find our darkness to be a part of the world's darkness. We have inherited it simply by being a part of the human race. We share also in the brokenness and "worldliness" in the Body of Christ, the Church.

But you and I are individual persons who have become what we are and what we will be through our actions upon and reactions to other individual persons. Our parents, friends, teachers, wife, husband, children, enemies and even "indifferent" acquaintances have helped to make us what we are by their attitudes, acts and even omissions. It is here that we come face to face with the *daimonic* in all of us, that which is part of our broken state of inauthenticity and also that which explains the good and the creative in our lives with its great potential for even such greater beauty in the future.

We can only grow in greater self-consciousness and hence in an awareness of ourselves as an individual "I," capable of self-giving in true love, by relationships with other centers of consciousness, able to call us into being by their love given freely to us. We grow in a *society*, a stable group of human beings in communication with each other. St. Paul could write: "The life and death of each of us has its influence on others" (Rm 14:7). Like Tennyson's *Ulysses*, in all of our travels from the first moment of waking consciousness until this moment and even to the end of our earthly existence, we can say: "I am a part of all that I have met."

This inter-dependence on others not only for our being but for our being such and such a person is testified by science. We inherit in birth not only the values of our parents but through them the values of generations and generations that preceded them. What an amazing world of inter-relationships science opens up to us through micro-biology. Each of the 100 trillion cells in your body contains about 100,000 different genes composed of *DNA* (deoxyribo-nucleic acid). Each *DNA* molecule stores coded information to be used to sustain and duplicate itself. Through such dependency upon our parents, we receive not only similar physical traits but we also are the recipients of much of their positive and negative qualities. We do share in their brokenness even before we see the light of day.

BORN TO BE NEUROTIC

S igmund Freud, the father of modern psychiatry, insisted on two elements. Unfortunately he claimed that there is no beginning to neurosis. To be born, for Freud, is to be already neurotic, since we have already been programmed by the hang-ups of our parents and their parents etc. His second conviction is equally devastating. The person who functions best in society is he who has built up the best *defense* against the attacks of others.

Such a teaching, I believe, is untenable for Christians who throughout all ages have believed both in the inter-dependence in brokenness, called "original sin" and also in the free will to opt with God's grace to become freed of such negative influences, not by defenses but by vulnerable love in self-giving to others.

In the next chapter we shall look at the healing power of love. Here we wish to take a hard look at our own brokenness. Seeing the magnitude of our own locked-in poverty, we will realize that we become healthy and integrated persons, not by defenses that we construct, but by God's healing love, administered often by other loving persons.

NEED FOR CARING PERSONS

You are born a creature of needs. You need food to sustain you in life. You need to be warm and kept clean and dry. You need to be surrounded by loving parents who hold you and caress you. You grow into self-awareness as they stimulate you through the sense of touch. When this latter is lacking, the child suffers pain. Two reactions follow. You will scream, cry, go into a tantrum of childish rage until you receive satisfaction. Or if you do not receive from your parents or those around you such physical signs of affection, you will seek to shut off the pain by suppressing the need.

Once, after a lecture to a group of charismatic leaders, a very successful, professional man came up to me. I knew him and his wife and so I gave him a warm embrace, an accepted way of greeting, especially among Christian charismatics. I felt his discomfort and I apologized. I was looking at the face of a little boy as I heard him say: "I only wish my father had done that to me when I was a kid!"

Not only had he been deprived of physical affection but his relationships toward his wife and his six grown children show a continued inability to express physically his true feelings for them. It is a most unhappy marriage. One grown boy is suicidal. Another is heavy into cocaine and alcohol. God means little to them and the four who are away from home have no desire ever to return.

This is brokenness! And how it is passed on from generation to generation and, yet, who is guilty?

THE UNREAL SELF

As a result of such needs unfulfilled in early childhood, all of us have suffered what Dr. Arthur Janov terms "the primal pains."[3] We ache in the depths of our consciousness and unconscious to have such basic needs satisfied. But worse, such pains create tensions and a split, according to Dr. Janov, between our *real* self, the subject of such desired needs, and our *unreal* self, that is created in defense to avoid greater pain. Dr. Janov writes:

> The child is born into his parents' needs and begins struggling to fulfill them almost from the moment he is alive. He may be pushed to smile (to appear happy), to coo, to wave bye-bye, later to sit up and walk, still later to push himself so that his parents can have an advanced child. As the child develops, the requirements upon him become more complex. He will have to get A's, to be helpful and do his chores, to be quiet and undemanding, not to talk too much, to say bright things, to be athletic. What he will not do is be himself . . . Each time a child is not held when he needs to be, each time he is shushed, ridiculed, ignored, or pushed beyond his limits, more weight will be added to his pool of hurts . . . As the assaults on the real system mount, they begin to crush the real person.[4]

The unreal self begins to emerge as the one that receives less of the hurts. But this self begins to grow farther away from the real self that becomes more and more suppressed into the unconscious. We struggle then to live according to our unreal self because such an approach to life is less painful. We forget what it feels like being spontaneous and free, because now we have lived so long with our false self that in our pained insecurity we fight to maintain that image of ourselves as our true, secured self.

This explains how very fiercely aggressive we can be when our unreal self is temporarily unmasked by others. We treat them who often truly love us as though they were our great enemies. This is seen often in the hate-love ambivalance found among married couples.

How uncomfortable and defenseless we feel in the impotence of serious sickness, above all, before death, or even in times of a spiritual retreat away from our habitual society and hence role-playing when our real self begins to show its head with a promise of what could be. Still we return sooner or later to ''normalcy'' and feel much better that things are as they always were.

FEARS

T he opposite of love, deeply received, will always be tensioned fears that build up in our lives as a result of not being able to grow into our true self spontaneously in the ambience of love freely given. When we lack the healing experience of true love, from God or fellow human beings, we lack a sense of our true identity, of our real self. Fear builds up and becomes centered in the apprehension of a future danger, unhappiness, doubt, anxiety, worry, dread, hatred, anger, horror, fright or terror. The thought of such impending evil weighs heavily upon our psyche and our body, crippling our growth, breaking down our health.

Fear can be about innumerable objects. It is the state of fear from which we must be delivered. From such brokenness we must be healed. And yet how deeply embedded into the fibers of our mind are the multitude of fears that hold us in slavery and a lack of freedom. One author describes some of these haunting fears that we are all only too familiar with.

> For example, our mothers stamp fear upon us before we are born, and continue to do it after we are born, and until we have grown old enough to fear for ourselves. They created disease for us through their fears of diseases until we get old enough to create our own diseases. And that wretched fear follows us from the cradle to the grave. We are afraid we shall not have the money to pay our bills for the current month and we generally lack something because we have created that lack. We fear bad luck, disaster and death, and it is a wonder that man has not swept himself off the face of the earth through his fearful creations.

The offspring of fear are the creatures and creations of this objective in mind, and the subjective mind which is within the objective mind accepts the unfortunate creations, believes the misrepresentations, and unites its own forces with those of the objective mind in bringing the pictured calamities into real external existence.[5]

NOT FREE TO LOVE

We crave above all else in life to love and to be loved. But pitifully the mounting rate of lonely persons committing physical or psychological suicides, the increase of broken marriages that end in divorce after divorce, the inability of so many parents to relate lovingly to their children and children to their parents, all point out how unfree we human beings are to love and receive love. What inner brokenness we experience in what God meant for us to be both the most human and divine experience, namely, in human love! We sincerely tell our loved ones that we really want to love them. But as we learn to enter into the depths of ourselves and the others, opening ourselves in all of our "unmasked" self, we experience fears and doubts. We find a true confrontation with our unredeemed, hidden areas that come out as we see ourselves being mirrored in the openness of the other. Demands of sensitivity and fidelity not known before are made in proportion as we receive the gift of the other. Self can no longer be the center, but we must seek humbly to serve only the unique godliness in the other. True love makes the awful demand on us to let the other be completely himself or herself. My selfish needs must yield to the godly desire to seek only to serve the uniqueness in the other, that which will fulfill the other's true self.

But what agony to let go and not hold on to the other! What a fear as my unreal self battles the hidden real self, as I struggle to "use" the other or die to the false in me to "serve" the other! I can so easily insist that the other person measure up to my expectations that means only all too often to satisfy my selfish needs. In my selfishness I can lose the "symbolic," that which integrates and binds into a oneness, and I, yield to the "diabolic," that which dis-integrates and scatters. I can lose the sense of wonder and mystery, poetry and going beyond my falsely constructed demands and insist that the other person be more the father or mother that I once needed to touch me and cuddle me.

A priest, ministering to people of all ages and backgrounds, sees much brokenness presenting itself to him for healing. Traveling all over America to preach retreats and lecture, I have met many persons, broken in body, soul, spirit. And yet so much brokenness was brought about often not because they deliberately willed to become broken. It is often a case of something happening to a given person, done by others who were equally caught in their own form of brokenness.

A beautiful husband and wife, after having six of their own children, decided to adopt an orphan boy, eighteen months old. The child was born of a Mexican mother who, while in a hospital for a nervous breakdown, was taken advantage of by her doctor. This boy was the result, born into a world of confusion, fear and insecurity. He is now twelve years old and in spite of all that the new parents and their children have done to make the adopted child wanted, he shows only hatred for them, especially toward the mother who so Christ-like had wanted him and loved him as her very own. That is brokenness!

I remember once meeting a man who was on the verge of a mental breakdown. He came to me in desperation. Although he was married and had seven children, he had a long history of homosexual relations with various men, starting with the priest that first initiated him as a young boy into such relations. He had gone to a psychiatrist who unraveled for him much of the brokenness between himself and his domineering mother. He married a woman that he expected to be just like his mother. And now he was afraid that his children would soon learn of his homosexuality. But what really bothered him was that he was to set-up housekeeping with a black man, unemployed and an alcoholic. When the latter did not get a job to support the two so the married man could give his salary to his wife and children, he was crushed and did not know which way to go. That is brokenness!

The nun, who as a child was molested by her uncle, is incapable of any deep, loving relationship with man or woman. That is brokenness! The list of broken people is endless. And, if you were to try to enumerate the number of similar cases, it would be endless. Yet each broken person would reveal to you and me something of our own brokenness. Is there no end to human brokenness? Is there a remedy?

THE PAIN OF PRAYER

H uman love is true prayer when we learn to die to our self-centeredness in order to open up to the creative presence of God in the other. But that is why in both true human love and prayer (can we truly separate the two?) there is so much necessary pain. In both, if there is to be any progress, there must be a touching of two centers of consciousness and this always means pain.

In prayer, especially, we are driven by God's Spirit into the barren desert of our inner self. Like Jesus Christ, we are to encounter the *daimonic* in us, both the horrible areas of darkness, fear, brokenness and the possibility of new, ressurrectional light, new life to come forth as creative energy released when the darkness is confronted.

It takes courage to go deeper into ourselves to confront the dark side. And for this reason the majority of us in prayer stay up "on top," in a very controlled relationship with God and the person that we think we are but that is not the real person that God wishes to love. We fear encountering so much ugliness in forms of darkness and distortion.

We fear the great temptation to push deeper into the unknown. Perhaps our small skiff on such troubled waters will easily capsize. Can we be sure that, going so deeply within us, we will be able to return? The line is very thin between madness and ecstatic union with God.

Farther into our brokenness we must go. The figures within us taunt us and attack us with a fierceness that breaks all of our ego-power. We feel helpless, trapped, surrounded by the most hideous enemies the human mind could ever imagine. Are they real or are they illusions? What is real and what is unreal? Jesus Christ, come to my rescue! Have mercy on me, the greatest of all sinners!

The false posturing before God, the grand soliloquies that I have been directing to the ear of God all fall from my heart as so many dry leaves falling from trees that in fall have no longer need for them. What I thought was important and significant in my life, fame, honor, pleasure, the joys shared with friends, all seem truly like straw. How unimportant they all seem! How unimportant I seem!

> What a wretched man I am. Who will rescue me from this
> body doomed to death? Thanks be to God through Jesus
> Christ our Lord! (Rm 7:24).

THE INNERMOST SELF

W hatever be the skein of knotted, twisted threads that have fashioned the tapestry of our lives (and so many of such influences were beyond our control), there lies deep within us another self, that true self of unrealized potentiality. In our brokenness we are driven into our creaturely nothingness. What can we do to extricate ourselves from the over-powering forces that have mostly come originally from without but now lie like unchained, wild dogs within us? Such a confrontation with our inner brokenness and nothingness before such overwhelming forces of negativity and destruction can be the turning point to a new life, a life of crying out for God's mercy and healing love.

Psychologist Dr. William Kraft speaks of our existential grasping of our nothingness in terms of loneliness, aloneness, depression, anxiety, guilt, frustration, anger, boredom, apathy and anguish.[6] Especially men and women in the middle-age of life can go through a crisis of limits where such a person:

> . . . feels intensely his limits, emptiness and negativity;
> and the positive and fulfilling meaning in life is something
> distant, foreign, and almost unreal. He feels that he really
> does not matter much to anyone or to himself. He feels
> like a zero—a nothing.[7]

Deep within us lies our real self, the person unrealized as yet, but loved infinitely by the triune God. God's Spirit hovers over this chaos, the darkness that could blaze forth into creative light, peace and joy if we would only stretch out and follow that thin, silvery streak of godly light out of the binding slavery into true freedom. It is here in our true self that God dwells, making His "mansion" (Jn 14:23) as we become more and more spirit communicating freely unto intimate loving communion with God's Spirit.

GOD'S HEALING LOVE

T o live on this level of loving union with the indwelling Trinity is to burst the bonds of pre-deterministic forces from within us and to step out of the cave of crippling, stifling darkness into the bright day of spring. Only God is powerful enough to aid us in becoming "re-born" again in His Holy Spirit of love (Jn 3:3-5). Only in experiencing the healing love from a tender, loving Father made manifest through the Spirit of the Risen Jesus can we rise from the brokenness of our past experiences to embrace new levels of a life in Christ, which is, as God always intended, to become our real self.

No longer do we have to be locked in the prison of our narcissism, to obey the dictates of others as the sole criterion of truth. Our habitual, low profile with all of our defenses to cover up our hurting inadequacies is replaced by an authentic humility that shows us from God's view our true self in the light of God's special gifts and endowments. Honesty and sincerity become like two bright shining beacons that dissipate any self-deceit from whatever cause.

This is a call to live in the freedom of the children of God. But it is a frightening call that demands daily courage to encounter the *daimonic* forces of darkness and of new potential far greater aliveness to God's loving presence everywhere. Dr. Carl Rogers describes this freedom:

> Freedom to be oneself is a frighteningly responsible freedom, and an individual moves toward it cautiously, fearfully, and with almost no confidence at first.[8]

It is within ourselves that we must enter in honesty and poverty of spirit that is the silence needed to hear God speak His still pointed Word. Into the tomb of our inner darkness, the light of God's tender love bursts upon us. Tears of sorrow and repentance, tears of fright at our own *non-being* pour forth gently as God's soft, healing dew falls upon the cracked, parched earth of our heart to stir those seeds of new life into reality.

As we utter the words: "Have mercy on me, O God, in your goodness" (Ps 51:1), we continually hear His healing response that thrills us into new life: ". . . this child of mine was dead and has come back to life; he was lost and is found" (Lk 15:24).

MEDITATION

DEEP DARKNESS

Father, frightened, Your child couches
In the depths of darkness and despair.

Fears and tremors, worries and cares
Attack him endlessly and he alone
Strikes now here, now there,
Only to be pummelled by invisible forces
Into hopeless prison-like confinement.

From whence these enemies come
To take me into everlasting servitude?
O bitter-day that I believed
His name *Lucifer* meant light-bearer
Instead of bearer of darkness and death!

Father, Your child is crying in the night
Because he thinks that he is all alone
In darkness and in fear. He does not know
That You are watching still. Send him Your Voice
To speak in stillness deep as summer fields
Kept windless in the blazing sun of noon
And silvered in the silence of the night,
But yet as loud as thunder. Tell him that
He need but turn to You and You will come
So swiftly he will instantly forget
The years or minutes his identity
In You was unremembered. Who could then
Recall the tiny ticks of time in which
The past went by; the fearful thoughts in which
The future was kept carefully concealed
In black unknowingness? Eternity
Has come to lift them both away and shine
In quiet certainty in place of time,
And all the little things that time must bring.
Look now upon the child who has forgotten
The meaning of Your love.

O holy Father of the universe,
Creator of all things that live in You,
In whom not one could ever be forgotten
Nor lost in time, the dreaming of the world
Will pass away with Your remembrance,
No child of Yours but must remember You.

Yet time must obscure eternity, as truth
Seems to be hidden when illusions rise
And veil the face of Christ. It does not seem
To have reality, and You who are
More near than breathing, yet appear to be
Remote; unreal, so far the distant stars
Seem closer. In long darkness it is hard
To keep the faith in the returning sun,
Your child is tired. Let him hear Your Voice,
and rest that sleep can never give be his.

Your child is sad. Remind him of Your Word,
And all the joy that suddenly becomes
Your gift to him is shared by all the world.
He is afraid. But let him hear the sound
Of Heaven's reassurance, and the years
Of almost hopeless waiting and despair
Shrink to a holy instant and be gone.

CHAPTER NINE

A HEALING SAVIOR

I n the popular musical, *Jesus Christ Superstar*, there is a dramatic scene in which the blind and the cripples, the lepers and the deformed, the dregs of society crawl out of the rocks and caves to surround and cover Jesus. As the broken ones of the world claw at Him, He cries out: "It's too much! There are too many of you!"

In the light of the great brokenness that we have seen in the world, even in Christ's Church, above all, in ourselves, we might be tempted to despair. There is just too much of evil in the world. There is this awful principle warring within my very members, seeking to destroy me (Rm 7:23)! Is there no light to dissipate the darkness? Is there no healing power that can bring new life to our broken bodies, souls, spirits?

For Christians Jesus Christ is the Way that heals the world of its brokenness. He has come among us in order to bring us life, that we might have it more abundantly (Jn 10:10). He inserted Himself into our broken, human condition in order that He might become one like us in all things save sin (Heb 4:15). More than becoming one like us, He remains always the Image of the Heavenly Father, one with Him in His Spirit of love. It is by His death on the cross that we can now believe in God's triune love for us individually.

> Yes, God loved the world so much
> that he gave his only Son,
> so that everyone who believes in him may not be lost
> but may have eternal life.
> For God sent his Son into the world
> not to condemn the world,
> but so that through him the world might be saved (Jn 3:16-17).

A HEALING SALVATION

W hen the writer of St. John's Gospel speaks of the world as being saved by the Son of God coming into the world, he is using the word *save* in the Semitic sense (the root word, *hajjim*) to describe fullness of happiness, joy and peace, total health, the result of living a full, good life under God's protection and within His holy will.

Such a healing salvation is to be an ongoing process as we confront courageously the brokenness within our own personal lives and around us within the various communities that fashion us into the persons we are. Such healing is a continued experience given us in prayer and in our loving service toward others by the Holy Spirit released in our hearts by the risen Jesus.

It is this loving Spirit that gives us an experience of God the Father's infinite love for us individually, made manifest to us by Jesus, who eternally is always dying for us. This Spirit allows us in our broken condition, irrespective of the causes that brought it about, to enter into a sharing in the crucifixion of Christ. In such darkness and apparent hopelessness, we can cry out in the Spirit's faith, hope and love that Jesus come to our rescue, save us and heal us.

This is the Good News that St. Paul experienced as he cried out in his brokenness: "What a wretched man I am! Who will rescue me from this body doomed to death? Thanks be to God through Jesus Christ our Lord!" (Rm 7:24). As he progressively suffered his brokenness as a sharing in Christ's crucifixion, so St. Paul experienced a healing unto new life in Jesus:

> I have been crucified with Christ, and I live now not with
> my own life but with the life of Christ who lives in me.
> The life I now live in this body I live in faith: faith in the
> Son of God who loved me and who sacrificed himself for
> my sake (Ga 2:19-20).

The Spirit's faith convinces us through God's revealed words in Holy Scripture that God in Jesus Christ wishes to forgive and heal all of our sins and diseases. Holy Scripture is not an account of how to rid society of each specific evil or sin or brokenness. It merely tells us that God wishes to heal all types of diseases, of psychic enslavement, of spiritual pride and complacency, in a word, to meet us in all of our brokenness and to restore His children to perfect health of body, soul and spirit.

JESUS WENT ABOUT HEALING

The New Testament community, as recorded especially in the four Gospels and the Acts of the Apostles, presents their belief that Jesus of Nazareth, who went about all of Palestine healing all those broken in body, soul or spirit who believed in His saving power, was still among them in His risen presence. In His believing members, Jesus was still bringing faith healings similar to those He wrought while He walked this earth.

These first believers of the Good News had seen Jesus, filled with the compassion of a mother for her suffering children, with the protective love of a shepherd for his sheep, with the total self-giving of a bridegroom for his bride, heal the multitude of sick persons brought to Him.

> He went round the whole of Galilee teaching in their synagogues, proclaiming the Good News of the kingdom and curing all kinds of diseases and sickness among the people.
> His fame spread throughout Syria, and those who were suffering from diseases and painful complaints of one kind or another, the possessed, epileptics, the paralyzed, were all brought to him and he cured them.
> He summoned his twelve disciples, and gave them authority over unclean spirits with power to cast them out and to cure all kinds of diseases and sickness.
> (Mt 4:23-24; 9:35; 10:1)

As in His lifetime, so now, Jesus, the reflected Image of the Father, is filled with love and compassion for all of us not yet freed from our broken enslavement to sin and death of any kind. We must first believe that He is still alive and living in His members, the Church, and that He truly wants to save us, to bring us into total healing of any and all forms of brokenness, as individuals and as corporate members of a society. We must give our lives to Him as to our Lord, by placing Him as center of all our desires and values instead of our selfish selves. We must forgive others and keep His commandments, especially that of loving one another as He loves us. As we grow in greater wholeness, He will work through us to bring healing to the world around us.

BROKEN DISCIPLES

We see how Jesus transformed His first disciples from broken, weak, sinful persons into healthy members of His Body, empowering them to be reconcilers of a separated, enslaved world into a loving, harmonious Church. In the *Acts of the Apostles* we see how Jesus' Spirit brought healing and freedom to Peter and the first called disciples.

How broken they were in their cowardliness to flee from their crucified Lord! How afraid they were to share in His sufferings! How proud they were in seeking power and honors as the main motives for following Jesus! But when the Spirit came upon Peter, he stood before the Jewish crowd and loudly proclaimed that Jesus was risen. Peter told them what they had to do to be rid of their brokenness: ''You must repent, and every one of you must be baptized in the name of Jesus Christ for the forgiveness of your sins, and you will receive the gift of the Holy Spirit'' (Ac 2:38).

A NEW CREATION

The Spirit gave power to Peter and John to stand before the Sanhedrin and boldly to proclaim that it is only through Jesus that there can be any true salvation, any total healing. ''For of all the names in the world given to men, this is the only one (the name of Jesus) by which we can be saved'' (Ac 4:12).

No longer afraid to suffer imprisonment and humiliations for the sake of their masters, these first disciples could bravely pray:

> 'And now, Lord, take note of their threats and help your
> servants to proclaim your message with all boldness, by
> stretching out your hand to heal and to work miracles and
> marvels through the name of your holy servant Jesus.' As

they prayed, the house where they were assembled rocked; they were all filled with the Holy Spirit and began to proclaim the word of God boldly (Ac 4:29-31).

Their powerful faith in the living, freeing power of Jesus' Spirit touched other believers and fashioned them into a believing and loving community. Bonds were broken that had earlier separated one from another. They gave themselves and their possessions to serve the Lord and to bring others into the freedom of children of God (Ac 2:37-47).

That community would spread throughout the then known world, bringing healing to the broken nations. No prisons, no threats, no enemies, not even death could take away the intoxicating freedom that those first Christians experienced in the risen Jesus and were able to share that freedom with others. Their brokenness had yielded to wholeness for they knew nothing could ever separate them from the love of God in Jesus Christ.

> Nothing therefore can come between us and the love of Christ, even if we are troubled or worried, or being persecuted, or lacking food or clothes, or being threatened or even attacked . . . These are the trials through which we triumph, by the power of him who loved us. For I am certain of this: neither death nor life, no angel, no prince, nothing that exists, nothing still to come, not any power, or height or depth, nor any created thing, can ever come between us and the love of God made visible in Christ Jesus our Lord (Rm 8:35-39).

NOT YET

The Christian communities found that daily they lived in the awful tension of having been healed of their brokenness and "not yet." As they opened up to new circumstances, they discovered new problem areas, a new need for healing both of new and old brokenness. Ananias and Sapphira "lied to the Holy Spirit" (Ac 5:3) in holding back money that they claimed they had given to the Jerusalem community. St. Peter and St. Paul confronted each other on the burning issue of whether Gentile converts had to submit to the Jewish laws of circumcision and purification.

St. Paul knew that he lived no longer he himself, but Jesus lived in him (Ga 2:20), yet he found that sin was still in his members (Rm 7:23). The Corinthians made up a temple in which the Spirit lived. Yet he had to admonish them for their lack of love toward each other, for dissensions, lust, covetousness, incest and a host of other indications of brokenness. He had to register pain and disappointment at the brokenness found among the Galatians as they followed false teachers and put their salvation in the law and not in Jesus and His Spirit who alone could pardon and heal them.

Loudly does St. Paul preach that only Jesus has the power to put to death the *old man* and to create the *new man*. The Spirit makes us into children of Abba, the Heavenly Father (Ga 4:6) and brings forth fruit that is totally different from the fruit of the worldly spirit (Ga 5:19-23).

St. Paul realized, as we all should, that Christians do not pass suddenly from the bondage of self-centeredness into the liberty of Christ. The full removal of all brokenness, sin and evil will come only in the freeing love of Christ's Spirit in the life to come. But, St. Paul's message is, that where Jesus' Spirit is, there is already liberty (2 C 3:17).

As we Christians permit this Spirit to act in our lives, He will transform us even now into the likeness of Jesus. Through that Spirit "the love of Christ overwhelms us" (2 C 5:14) as we reflect that He died "so that living men should live no longer for themselves but for him who died and was raised to life for them" (2 C 5:15).

HEALING OF THE PAST

This loving Jesus who lives within us is capable of healing our brokenness that rears its ugly hydra heads out of the past from out of our repressed hurts and fears of the ghosts of yester-years. We need no longer be slaves of the past, of our sins and failures, of the seething hurts and angers because of what others have done to us. There is only this present moment as the Holy Spirit rips off the false posturing and phony masks that have created an illusion out of the past.

No matter how much we have been hurt and deformed in past events, the Spirit pours the love of God into our hearts (Rm 5:5). In a gentle security of knowing we are loved by the all-perfect God, we let go of our need to interpret events or happenings of the past according to our darkened ideas that we entertain, especially of our false *ego*. Not having had a true love of ourselves because our faith was not strong enough in the past to convince us of God's infinite love for us unto death in His Son Jesus, we fashioned opinions of ourselves and the world around us that were simply lies and did not present the "really real" as God sees it.

What healing of life's past hurts can come from experiencing this personalized love of a triune God that dwells within us! Such healing can come daily as we sit deeply in prayer and allow God's love to heal past brokenness. It can come through healing in a praying group as we join our faith to that of loving Christians who bring the powerful intercession of Jesus, the High-Priest, to intercede with the Father to remove any brokenness and bring us into a oneness with Him and a oneness with the Body of Christ. It can come also in deep healing as we receive the sacraments of the Church and encounter again the living Jesus in His Body bringing us into a new-founded wholeness as we believe in His saving presence.

What a gift we should find in the sacrament of reconciliation as we submit the hurts of the past to the present love of the Savior, Jesus Christ! But above all, what healings of past hurts can come to us as we receive the Eucharist, the Body and Blood of Jesus! No matter how great should be the brokenness in our own individual lives and in our community in which we live, the Eucharist is the new Covenant whereby God continually gives His blood for the remission of sins, the removal of our brokenness and for the life of the world (Heb 9:15; 9:25-28).

In our oneness with Jesus Christ in the Eucharist we are brought into the heart of the Trinity. Here is the climax of God's eternal plan when He "chose us in Christ to be holy and spotless, and to live through love in his presence" (Ep 1:4). Our past sinfulness, added to the effects of the sin of the world, hindered the Holy Spirit from raising us to an awareness in grace that Jesus truly lived in us and we in Him. But in the Eucharist, if we are truly repentant and aware of our need for healing in an authentic *metanoia* or conversion, the Spirit of Jesus restores and powerfully builds up this oneness with Jesus Christ and His Heavenly Father.

It is especially in the reception of the Eucharist that all members of Christ's Body are most powerfully united in a new sense of oneness with each other. It is this union that breaks down the separation and division that have caused so much brokenness in our past lives. But such brokenness that in the past has separated us from other human beings is overcome in the Eucharist by the divinizing power of the Trinity experienced as the power that drives us outward toward other communities to be Eucharist, bread broken, to give ourselves, not only as Jesus did on our behalf, but with Jesus and the Father abiding within us with their Spirit of love empowering us to do that which would be impossible for us alone to do consistently.

HEALING OF FUTURE BROKENNESS

B ecause of our basic lack of faith, hope and love shown toward God in the present moment that is the only "place" where we can open ourselves to God's healing love, we project the brokenness of the past and the present into the future. Fears of all sorts, as laughing specters, haunt us, as soon as we open the window that looks onto tomorrow. We fear the loss of our health, our job. Future dangers of all sorts rise up in our imagination to petrify us into inactivity. We fear death. We fear inflation. We fear muggings and robberies. We fear car accidents and air crashes. Fears mount and soon we are fearing our fears.

Fears of future evils spawn various other forms of brokenness. We worry about and dread certain situations. We fear and suspect others who soon become our enemies, even among those who truly love us. We withdraw from their company or we become aggressive toward them each time we are about to meet them.

We can be healed of future brokenness only by accepting fully the present moment as an exciting gift from God. By opening ourselves in complete, child-like trust and abandonment to God's loving, creative presence in this now moment, we move away from the unreal past and the illusory future that we have created to enter into God's real next step where we will find Him loving us in our brokenness and weakness and becoming our future strength.

A HEALING FAITH

I t is not enough to believe in our own weakness and brokenness and to believe that God is present as loving us in each present moment. By the faith of the Spirit of the risen Jesus we "see" God in each moment, in each event. We stretch out, beyond our own limited gaze of what is possible, to get in touch with God's loving activities and then we work to effect a transformation to something better. God heals us as we cooperate to work for a new creation. Faith illumines us in a freeing way to see God inside of the present moment. But this brings by faith a freeing from ourselves and the limitations that we place upon ourselves and upon others. The negativity that believes we and others can do only so much is transcended by faith so that we can truly shout out to ourselves and to the whole world: "I can do all things in Him who strengthens me."

We do not recklessly presume that God will do all things while we sit back in our brokenness to expect a miracle or a mighty sign to prove that with God all things are possible. We seek through discernment of the true Spirit an authentic assessment of the given situation and what we can do with God's help to change matters according to God's will. We humbly see the situation through faith and share somewhat, at least in our desire, in God's appraisal of the event. We may turn the other cheek when an enemy smotes us on one cheek, but we know also that God would want us to work diligently at the same time to transform the enemy by our love and prayerful intercession into our brother. Faith works along with God's gift of human intelligence, but it allows us to see farther into the tunnel when our own human knowledge runs out of light.

GOD'S WORD

T he Christian believes that he or she can encounter the healing Jesus through an inner discipline of listening to Him as the living Word of God breaks in upon the believer that enlightens, guides, nourishes and sets him or her free. Jesus spoke about the freeing power of the Word:

> If you make my word your home
> you will indeed be my disciples,
> you will learn the truth
> and the truth will make you free (Jn 8:31-32).

The Word of God is "something alive and active; it cuts like any double-edged sword but more finely . . . No created thing can hide from him; everything is uncovered and open to the eyes of the one to whom we must give account of ourselves" (Heb 4:12-13). Praying over the words of Holy Scripture gives birth in our hearts to deeper faith, hope and love. The Spirit of Jesus gives us new understanding and knowledge of the Word. In that word, we can pray with St. Paul that we, too, may "know Christ and the power of his resurrection and to share his sufferings by reproducing the pattern of his death" (Ph 3:10).

To *know* Jesus Christ in Scripture is to move into a perfect union in love where two wills become one. To know Him in this sense is to open ourselves to His dynamic leadership at each moment. It is to experience, that in spite of our brokenness, we are loved infinitely by Him. We know that we know that we know that Jesus loves us, even though we are completely unworthy of this honor. We can never know why or how this happens. But His Spirit fills us with this knowledge that surpasses all human understanding. It is to know that you are "planted in love and built on love . . . until, knowing the love of Christ, which is beyond all knowledge, you are filled with the utter fullness of God" (Ep 3:17-19).

He is our Lord and He can command anything. We hold ourselves in complete obedience to His word, for His love calls out from our hearts a similar love response that must be measured, if it is to be true love, by a loving submission to obey His every wish. Such a knowledge inundates our whole being, soaking our mind, our will, our emotions and even our body with His loving presence.

To experience His resurrection is to know, in spite of our brokenness and even sinful tendencies, that He has conquered sin and death and His resurrection is already given to us. "Children, you have already overcome these false prophets, because you are from God and you have in you one who is greater than anyone in this world" (1 Jn 4:4).

To share in the sufferings of Jesus is not only to accept our present brokenness within ourselves and in the world around us but actively to discipline ourselves to nail our false selves to the cross in order that through such a death to self He may triumph in us and even now share with us His eternal life. It means entering into the combat against the demonic forces within us and around us, everywhere in the world. We are called to be soldiers and athletes, to use St. Paul's metaphors, as we discipline our bodies and our senses, our interior faculties of intellect, emotions and will, so that we can become truly attentive to God's Word and become supple instruments for Him to use in reconciling the whole world to His Father.

LOVED AND HEALED

In such inner attentiveness to the darkness and brokenness within myself, I allow Jesus and His Father to cover me with their tender yet powerful, everlasting love. I am loved by God! No matter how great is my brokenness, from whatever past or future cause, one thing I am certain of. God loves me! God in Jesus dies for me! God cares for me! I am broken but loved! In such love brokenness is transformed into a new life in Christ as I stretch out still more to possess that love. Strangely now, my weakness becomes my strength before God's compassion and mercy. The knowledge of my true state of brokenness now leads me to a knowing of God's love that makes such knowledge true love.

Is there in this life any other way to experience the true love of God except in the contrast of our brokenness? How can God heal us by His love if we have not been broken in our ignorance of not having been loved by Him and others? How can we understand what God's presence means unless we have experienced His absence? How can we experience the Prodigal Father unless we first have experienced what a prodigal son or daughter means?

MEDITATION

BROKEN BUT LOVED

I join the crowd of broken people,
hobbling, falling, screaming and crying

in their sickness and inner misery.
Frantically we search now here now there.
Can no one heal us, bring us new life?
We hang on each other and we pull each other down
into a sharing of misery added to each other's.

What darkness covers my soul!
What bonds hold me imprisoned!
What leprous wounds cover me
and eat my substance away!

O Jesus, Divine Physician, come
and stretch Your healing hands upon me.
Break loose my bonds and set me free.
Dispel the darkness by the light of Your presence.
Thaw the freezing in all my limbs.
Warm my cold isolation with Your love.

O most gentle, merciful Savior,
bend over me again and enspirit
these dry bones of mine
with Your Spirit that alone brings new life.
Let me feel once more Your healing touch,
that resurrects me from the dead,
that quiets the storm within my breast.
Let Your love sear through me
like an arrow plunged deep down
into the last resistance in my heart.

Lord and Master, how great is Your love,
how ever abiding and everlasting
and, yet, how blinded I was to Your great light,
how absent to Your surrendering presence.

I cry out, Savior, that You offer again
that healing love that destroys all sin,
that breaks down prison walls of pride
and sends me forth in humble service
to share Your healing love with others.

"Here is My love offered to you,
a love of pain, suffering unto death.

Take and receive My gift of Self,
My healing stillness that drives
from out your heart all noise and clamor,
My whispering love that shouts to you
of love divine, pursuing, ever present.

This healing love I give to you.
Kneel down to receive this anointing
as kings of old, as consecrated priests.
I send you forth, healed and whole
to be a healing touch of love
to all you meet.
You were broken, but always loved.
Now be love to those who still know
not of My healing, loving power.
Tell them the Good News
that darkness can be turned into light,
loneliness can embrace and be united
into a loving community of many
in the oneness of My love.
Absence is driven out by presence,
brokenness can be healed by love!

CHAPTER TEN

A BROKEN HEALER

I n spite of ever increasing problems that cover our universe like a black, suffocating cloud of despair, God is doing a great thing. Many Christians, who have been nominal believers in Jesus Christ for so much of their lives, are being moved by the Holy Spirit to discover Jesus in the Gospels. The Good News that He preached and brought about by His healing love is being freshly experienced today by ordinary persons. Housewives, truck drivers, farmers, office workers, teachers and religious nuns, ministers and priests are finding out that God's Word is for them and precisely in the context of their daily lives.

It is exciting to see, amid so much brokenness around us, such ordinary persons coming alive by a new founded faith in the power of the risen Jesus. He is truly Lord! In Him we live and move and have our being (Ac 17:28). With Him all things are possible for He is yesterday, today and always the same almighty, loving Lord. Such Christians cry out for a deeper faith. "I do have faith. Help the little faith I have!" (Mk 9:24).

They have meditated and then have begun to act on the words from the New Testament that have come from the mouth of Jesus:

> I tell you solemnly, if you have faith and do not doubt at
> all, not only will you do what I have done to the fig tree,
> but even if you say to this mountain, "Get up and throw
> yourself into the sea," it will be done. And if you have
> faith, everything you ask for in prayer you will receive
> (Mt 21:21-22).

Like little children, they trust in the words of the Lord. They act before a doubting world and confess in word and deed that Jesus Christ is true God and true Man. He is Lord and Master in their lives. They believe that their Lord is risen and lives among them when two or three gather in His name. They believe that their Lord can do all things and from Holy Scripture they believe that He wishes to heal all men. As they have received the highest healing in an ongoing process of ever increasing growth of faith in their spirit, they turn their lives over to Him to let Him minister His healing to others through them as channels. Their only wish is that God be glorified. They are nothing without Christ. He is the Vine, and they are mere branches that bring to other branches the life giving energy of God's love that courses through their beings (Jn 15).

And that is why they can pray without any hesitation for they truly believe that God is a healing God, "Rapha-el," the one who heals (Ex 15:26-27). "But he must ask with faith, and no trace of doubt . . . That sort of person, in two minds, wavering between going different ways, must not expect that the Lord will give him anything" (Ja 1:6-8). Jesus constantly recalls to their minds what He had said:

> I tell you therefore: everything you ask and pray for,
> believe that you have it already, and it will be yours. And
> when you stand in prayer, forgive whatever you have
> against anybody, so that your Father in heaven may for-
> give your failings too (Mk 11:24-25).

GOD NEEDS YOU

We have already pondered the awesome mystery of God's humility. We can understand Him as the fullness of perfection, immutable and unchangeable. We can believe that He loves us. We can even believe that His love for us is infinite and everlasting. But we will always be thrown down to our knees in humble adoration as we ponder, from God's revealed words in Scripture, that God truly wants our love. He waits with longing for our response to His invitation.

Yet God's waiting, His reaching out to touch us and receive our response to His covenant-love is linked to other human beings. God gave Himself to a whole people through Abraham's *faithful* surrender.

The Israelites were freed from slavery because God needed Moses to respond to His invitation to go down to Egypt and set His people free. They were purified through the intercession of Moses on behalf of his stiff-necked people. God "localized" Himself in the Ark of the Covenant, but the Israelites had to carryHis presence with them into battle and before every great need.

God "needed" prophets, kings and judges to call His people back to Him. Jeremiah is the model prophet who would portray the need of God for His greatest Prophet, Jesus Christ, His only Son, to bring His message to His people. Jeremiah pleaded with God, even though he felt it was hopeless, so hardened had the Jewish people become. He suffered with God rejection from the people. "Realize that I suffer insult for your sake" (Jr 15:15 b). Still Jeremiah seemingly felt his responsibility to stand before his people and call them back to repentance. "Wash your heart clean of wickedness, Jerusalem, and so be saved" (Jr 4:14).

A NEEDED INCARNATION

B ut when the Word becomes flesh and dwells among us, we at last see God's crying need for "another," not only to speak His message but to be the very message, the very Word of God Himself in human form. When we read those stirring words: "God loved the world so much that he gave his only Son so that everyone who believes in him may not be lost . . ." (Jn 3:16), we begin to understand something about the pursuing love of God as he truly seeks our human response. Jesus became sin for our sakes that we might be delivered from sin. He becomes the greatest of all prophets and high priests since He literally stands between God and man. He stands before His eternal Father in perfect, self-surrendering love. But He also stands among us, lives within us and gives Himself in perfect self-surrendering love to draw out of us a similar love.

He is the ultimate High-Priest because He not only offers the victim but He is the victim. He is the Priest that offers and He is also the gift offered.

> He brings a new covenant, as the mediator, only so that
> the people who were called to an eternal inheritance may

actually receive what was promised; his death took place
to cancel the sins that infringed the earlier covenant (Heb
9:15).

NEED FOR DISCIPLES

Yet God in Jesus still had need of other human beings to extend the
prophetic preaching of Jesus and His priesthood to all nations.
For three years Jesus formed twelve Apostles into a very special
group. He taught them and other disciples and sent them to preach His
message. He empowered them to announce the Kingdom of God
through the Good News. But He gave them also power to heal the
broken ones that they met. They were promised by Jesus that they
would do even greater things than He did (Jn 14:12-13).

> Go out to the whole world; proclaim the Good News to all
> creation. He who believes and is baptised will be saved;
> he who does not believe will be condemned. These are the
> signs that will be associated with believers: in my name
> they will cast out devils . . . they will lay their hands on the
> sick, who will recover (Mk 16:16-18).

And they did go out, down through the ages, an army of believing
disciples of Jesus. They prayed over the sick and people were healed.
St. Peter had only to walk among the beds and mats placed in the
streets of Jerusalem and his shadow, falling upon the sick, was enough
that "all of them were cured" (Ac 5:16). Others have followed the
first Apostles and allowed themselves to become channels for the
healing power of Jesus to be extended into the brokenness of all ages.
Through the touch of medical doctors and nurses, through the anointing hand of the priest in the sacrament for the sick, through the hand
lifted in absolution or in giving the Bread of Life, Jesus has continued
to destroy sin and death, brokenness in this world and to bring about a
"new creation."

INTERCESSORS

One of the most important ways all Christians are called to be a
healing force in a broken world is through intercessory prayer.

An ancient Chinese proverb says: "It is better to light one candle than to curse the darkness." Knowing that Jesus Christ alone is the High Priest and sole Intercessor before the throne of the Father, yet each Christian also realizes the call by Baptism to have a share in that priesthood. Jesus alone offers up the pleasing sacrifice to God (Heb 7:26-27). But we are called also to share in that priestly action.

> . . . set yourselves close to him so that you too, the holy priesthood that offers the spiritual sacrifices which Jesus Christ has made acceptable to God, may be living stones making a spiritual house . . . But you are a chosen race, a royal priesthood, a consecrated nation, a people set apart to sing the praises of God who called you out of darkness into his wonderful light (1 P 2:5, 9).

Some are given the special charism to be cultic priests, ordained to renew the sacrifice of Christ and visibly to gather up the sacrifices of the Church that obeys His command to do this action in His memory. But all Christians, regardless of their state of life, sex, education, health or any other factor, are called in Baptism to bring the mediating presence of Jesus Christ into their place and time in history. "It was God who reconciled us to himself through Christ and gave us the work of handing on this reconciliation" (2 Co 5:18).

We are called into the work of combatting any brokenness and separation by bringing the reconciling, redemptive work of Jesus Christ into the small area of human existence that God has given us to work upon. It is indeed awesome to think that God has chosen us and placed us into a certain part of the whole world that is groaning in its imperfect state of brokenness in order that through our intercession the presence of the healing Jesus may again be felt in the suffering world.

But this brings with it an equal responsibility to become purified so that the presence of Jesus may shine through to those who lie in darkness. As we have become healed of our brokenness, purified in heart, then Jesus will use us to become transforming, healing love toward all whom we meet. We may never have the consolation of seeing the terribly sick and broken in body or spirit rise under our touch to be healed by the power of Jesus working so directly through us. But all of us in deep faith and humility can give ourselves to be points through which Jesus again encounters the brokenness of our human society and effects a reconciliation.

We have it in our prayerful power to bring Jesus to the many dead Lazaruses in our neighborhoods, cities, states and countries. We can weep over the spiritual tepidity and even spiritual death of so many living around us. Like Moses, we can burn with zeal for the salvation of our brothers and sisters as we stand with outstreched arms pleading before God for their salvation. Like St. Paul, we wish rather not to enter into the Kingdom of Heaven if it would mean being separated from our suffering brothers and sisters and giving up the possibility of helping them come into full health.

Especially in the quiet of night when darkness seems to stop the rapid flow of time, you are able to bring the healing power of the risen Lord to any part of the world. You can be present by love to the suffering and dying Cambodians in their refugee camps. You have the power in intercessory prayer to enter into concentration camps in the U.S.S.R. and bring solace and a freeing of the hearts of those captives from oppression. You can be at the bedside of the suffering and dying in hospitals all over the world, releasing the healing love of the Trinity into their pain-wracked bodies. The mentally deranged and depressed you can cover with the calming love of Jesus.

LOVE BEGETS LOVE

God extends His healing love to others by pouring His trainitarian love into your heart. It is a powerful but gentle love that permeates and invades your being at all times. True contemplation becomes an ever increasing consciousness of this exuberant, out-pouring love of God as God reveals His energetic love for you in each moment of each event.

As you allow God's love to flow over you like life-giving water, cleansing you of your locked-in self-centeredness, you become transformed into a loving person, open to give love to all whom you meet. A strange paradox becomes a daily experience. As God's love is brought to life within you and experienced in a new awareness of your identity in being loved so richly and exuberantly by God as Father, Son and Holy Spirit, so you are "impelled" by that inner force of the indwelling Spirit to bring forth by your love for your neighbor God's healing love in the other.

In my room I have a banner that summarizes this godly-begetting love:

> In loving one another,
> God in us is made flesh.

FASTING

B ut true Christian love is proved by deeds. "A man can have no greater love than to lay down his life for his friends" (Jn 15:13). It can be a real deception of our intercession, on behalf of our brothers and sisters, suffering in body, soul or spirit brokenness, if limited only to prayers said on their behalf. Our true, healing love must have a quality before God and neighbor of sincerity and generosity. God's love in us as shown by the sufferings and death of Jesus unto the last drop of blood, drives us also to embrace the cross of creative suffering as a sign of pure love and complete self-sacrifice.

One powerful, intercessory prayer is an action—that of Christian fasting. There are many motives why we may wish to fast. One that the Church has constantly stressed is the power of fasting as intercessory prayer when the Holy Spirit inspires us to enter into God's merciful forgiveness and healing love.

Such fasting on behalf of the others must be an act of God-inspired love that we offer to God from our humble and contrite heart. It must be the Holy Spirit who inspires us to fast out of a love that He is pouring into our hearts for others. It is going "another mile" (Mt 5:42), sheerly out of love for another and not out of the obligation of justice.

God is surely not pleased with the suffering that we experience in fasting. He sees the love that is symbolized by an action that does not take our life away but it brings us close at least to experiencing a death-like abnegation of our instinct for self-preservation. It is a free will act to want on behalf of our neighbor to suffer something of the cross of Christ in order to apply the intercession of Jesus to the brokenness of the neighbor. It is St. Paul's desire to become a Jew to the Jew, weak to the weak, in order to win them all to Christ.

Such freely chosen "creative suffering" can have a great efficacy, in the Church's teaching on the communion of Saints, to apply Christ's healing power to effect a healing for those to whom we direct our creative suffering. Such creative suffering goes far beyond any mere fasting from food to embrace any time of self-abnegation out of love for God and neighbor.

MONOTONY OF LOVE

In God's divine providence He has directed us, through free choices made by others in our regard and made by ourselves, into a community. We were born not by our choice but by choices made by our parents. Our family situation is something presented to us. Usually it is there that we are to receive our first healings unto new life by the love of our parents given to us gradually and, hopefully, continually. It is there that we are to respond to their love and that of others in that family by the gift of ourselves to them.

At the heart of such familial love, the primal experience for us of the healing power of love, is its constancy. In season and out of season, in high and low moments, when we feel like it or not, we are driven to respond in love. It is in the very monotony and sameness of family love that we become true lovers who with purified hearts learn gradually to love without counting the cost, without seeking some personal return.

This is healing love that ever so gradually over long, slow years draws our loved ones into a sense of their true worth and uniqueness as persons. When this healing love is consistently and deeply experienced in family life, it will allow us to go beyond the family into our schools, churches, market places and daily work to carry such healing love to others. Our society is a mere reflection of how healed individual members have become in their families.

LAYING ON OF HANDS

We minister healing love to others around us by showing that we care for them. But true caring always is a basic movement or gesture of pouring ourselves outwardly *toward* others in their needs. Hands have been given us to touch others and assure them that we do care for them. Arms have been given to surround and soothe in loving embrace. To touch another in love is to break down artificial walls and to drive away fears and suspicions from the other. It is the way human beings and animals communicate a caring, healing love.

We are not surprised when we see in the Gospels that Jesus often laid His hands upon the broken in body and spirit and they received in that gesture His healing love. He taught His disciples to go forth throughout the whole world and do likewise.

> Go out to the whole world, proclaim
> the Good News to all creation . . . they
> will lay their hands on the sick,
> who will recover (Mk 16:16-18).

The early Christians believed in praying over each other in sickness. Those strong in faith, as St. James writes, were to anoint the sick person "with oil in the name of the Lord and pray over him" (Jm 5:14). For many centuries lay persons blessed oil and used it to anoint the sick or disturbed in their families as they laid hands on them to bring the healing love of Jesus to them.

Today many Christians, with new-founded faith, are praying Holy Scripture. They are acting on the belief that where two or three gather in the name of Jesus, there He is among them (Mt 18:20), bringing His healing power again to the broken ones of this world. They are experiencing that persons are being healed on all levels of body, psychic and spiritual disturbance when they themselves pray over the sick. They humbly beg Jesus to use their hands to communicate His healing love again to the broken ones of this world.

HEALING OF THE SPIRIT

For such Christians of child-like faith in the compassionate mercy and love of Jesus Christ, He is still operating through believers in His powerful presence when they pray over others in His name. They pray without wavering. They possess a child-like confidence that God will always heal. But they know healing is never only on the physical level. They lead the sick and broken to share in their faith vision of God's loving goodness.

God always does heal by pouring an infusion of deeper faith, hope and love into the needy person if we find the proper dispositions. Healing must always begin on the spiritual level of a healing of one's weak faith in the love of God for that person. The complete manifestation of healing on the psychic or physical level is left in trusting abandonment to God's holy designs. For this reason such Christian healers can lead the sick, who are prayed over, into a deeper faith that allows them to expect that God will always heal, at least on the spiritual plane, all who call upon the Father in the name of Jesus Christ.

Christianity spread so rapidly in the ealry Church, not because of worldly wisdom or even methods on the social level to change society with new structures, but because of the child-like faith of Christians who had turned their lives over to God and who lived radically the Gospel through a living faith in the healing power of God.

BROKEN HEALERS

We have striven to present in the preceding chapters the theme of brokenness. We in no exhaustive manner showed some of the brokenness of our world. Jesus entered into that brokenness in order to struggle with it and conquer it by His Spirit of love. He broke the back of "sin and death" when He *passed over* in His act of perfect love for the Heavenly Father and for you and me.

We confronted something of the awful contagion of sin that has brought so much disharmony and fragmentation into our world. We saw the brokenness in the Church, the very Body of Christ. And we pondered how we ourselves also are broken in so many ways. We profess that Jesus truly can and wants to heal us. And thus daily we cry out for His healing love to touch the roots of our inauthentic selves and lead us into a sharing in His life.

To the degree that He heals us as we experience God's infinite love made manifest to us through Jesus in His Holy Spirit, we are impelled to open up to each person that we encounter. Jesus wants to extend His conquering power over the brokenness of this world through persons like you and me. We have been broken and healed by His love. We can say that also in other ways we are still broken and are in need of His healing power.

Yet as broken, loved and healed, we have the awesome responsibility to extend Jesus, the Healer, into the world around us. As we lovingly care for others, we let the healing power of God pour into their lives. Yet we also, paradoxically, called to bring healing to the brokenness in others, experience an increase in new healing love turned toward our own brokenness.

A process goes on, both in this life and in the life to come, of being healed of the brokenness of the world that has become a part of our experience so as to be able to love others more. As we do give ourselves in unselfish service, we lead them out of their isolation and self-centeredness. But in that process we become healed a bit more of our brokenness and alienation. We become, then, capable of bringing more of Jesus' healing love to others, thus extending the conquest of Jesus as Reconciler of all things to His Father.

There is hope for this mad world of ours. Its filth, sordidness and seeming absurdity, its brokenness and evil, sin and death can be not only overcome by God's love in Jesus and His Spirit but can be transformed into a "new creation" (2 C 5:17). God needs human beings, broken but healed, to extend His healing love that alone, as light can dispel the darkness that covers our world in meaninglessness. Only love can heal and make new; but God extends His love through you and me into this world.

> And for anyone who is in Christ, there is a new creation;
> the old creation has gone, and now the new one is here. It
> is all God's work. It was God who reconciled us to himself
> through Christ and gave us the work of handing on this
> reconciliation. In other words, God in Christ was recon-
> ciling the world to himself, not holding men's faults
> against them, and he has entrusted to us the news that they
> are reconciled. So we are ambassadors for Christ; it is as
> though God were appealing through us, and the appeal
> that we make in Christ's name is: be reconciled to God.
>
> (2 C 5:17-20)

MEDITATION

I walked along the quiet mountain road.
The full moon laughed with joy
while the rest of nature slept.
I entered into a crevice
of a rock near the stream.

There was peace.
But then I felt God's presence
slowly come upon me.
Faster and faster He pursued me.
I wasn't running from Him.
I was entering *into* Him!

Deeper and deeper
I plunged!
I knew that somehow
when I left this place
I would always remain
in that crevice,
so full of God's peace and joy.

I had touched God
I found Heaven on earth!
God's Spirit had come upon me
in that moonlit evening
As I hid in the arms
of God, my Beloved!

Oh, what healing love
comes over my brokenness!
All healing comes from God
in the desert cave
when I in brokenness
call out to You, Divine Physician.

I will never be the same
since You touched me
and I hid in Your healing arms.

New powers awake
as spring-clarion sounds
within the depths of that crevice,
the rock of my heart.

Locked-in petals
of a be-dewed rose
gently let go
to unveil a new harmony
of many things captured
in the union of one flower
of exquisite beauty.

The chaotic past, dried bones
of long yester-years,
receive the soft breath
of God's Spirit of Love.

And they became enfleshed
into a living being.
I come out of the past
as I cry to my Lord,
"Lord, Jesus Christ, Son of God,
have mercy on me
a sinner!"

Like butterfly bursting
forth in melted gold
with wet, tightly-packed wings,
I stretch upward.
Dry wings strengthen
and lift me aloft
to new, dizzying heights
of union with God.

But then I hear
that healing voice
say to me,
"Go to your broken
brothers and sisters.

Stretch out your hands
on their pain-ridden bodies.

Give My healing love
to all that you meet.
Be My hands and feet
that again can like Shepherd
gather the scattered sheep
and bring them to My Father."

Broken but healed,
I step out in faith
to be a broken healer
to a broken world.

CHAPTER ONE
FOOTNOTES

1. On this theme cf.: Eulalio R. Baltazar: *The Dark Center. A Process Theology of Blackness* (N.Y.: Paulist Press, 1973)
2. Thierry Maertens: *Bible Themes, Vol. 1 (Bruges: Biblica*, 1964) p. 51.
3. Abraham Heschel: *The Prophets* (N.Y.: Harper & Row, 1971) Vol. 2, ch. 1, passim.
4. On the biblical concept of God as vulnerable, cf.: Burton Z. Cooper: *The Idea of God* (The Hague: M. Nynoff, 1974) p. 5.
5. Meister Eckhart; ed. Franz Pfeiffer; tr. C. de B. Evans (London: Watkins, 1947) Vol. 1, p. 267.
6. On this subject, cf.: Jurgen Moltmann: The Crucified God (N.Y.: Harper & Row, 1973) pp. 202 ff.
7. Gerald Vann, O. P.: *The Pain of Christ and the Sorrow of God* (London: Blackfriars, 1947) pp. 67-69.
8. Jurgen Moltmann, *op. cit.* p. 243.

CHAPTER TWO
FOOTNOTES

1. Elie Wiesel: *Night* (Avon, 1969) p. 75.

CHAPTER SIX
FOOTNOTES

1. T.S. Eliot: *Murder in the Cathedral*, in: *The Complete Poems and Plays* (N.Y.: Harcourt, Brace & Co., 1930) p. 180.
2. R.L. Heilbroner: *An Inquiry Into the Human Prospect* (N.Y.: W.W. Norton, 1974) pp. 16, 18-19.
3. Ibid., pp. 32-34.
4. Karl Menninger: *Whatever Became of Sin?* (N.Y.: Hawthorn Books, Inc., 1973) p. 13.
5. A. Hulsbosch: *God's Creation* (N.Y.: Sheed & Ward, 1965) p. 56.
6. Cf.: Irving L. Janis: "Groupthink" in: *Psychology Today*, November, 1971, vol. 5:43.

CHAPTER SEVEN
FOOTNOTES

1. F.X. Durrwell, C.SS.R.: *The Resurrection*, tr. Rosemary Sheed (N.Y.: Sheed & Ward, 1966) pp. 1-34.
2. St. Cyprian: *De Oratione Dominica*, 23: *PL* 4:553.
3. Cf.: H. De Lubac, S.J.: *The Splendor of the Church*, tr. Michael Mason (N.Y.: Sheed & Ward, 1956). pp. 69-71.
4. Alfred Whitehead: *Process and Reality* (N.Y.: Macmillan, 1929) pp. 519-520.

5. Letter to the bishops, dukes and counts of Germany, Sept. 3, 1076, as quoted by Yves Congar, O.P.: *Power and Poverty in the Church*, tr. Jennifer Nicholson (Baltimore: Helicon, 1964) p. 105.
6. St. Bernard: *De Consideratione*, IV, 3, 6; *PL* 182, 776A, cited by Yves Congar, op. cit., p. 125.
7. St. Hilary of Poitiers: *The Trinity*, tr. Stephen McKenna, C.SS.R., in: *The Fathers of the Church* (N.Y., 1954) Vol. 25, p. 36.

CHAPTER EIGHT
FOOTNOTES

1. R. Maria Rilke: Letter 74, *Briefe aus den Jahren 1907 bis 1914*, cited by Rollo May: *Love and Will* (N.Y.: Dell Publishing Co., Inc. 1969) p. 122.
2. Op. cit., p. 139.
3. Arthur Janov: *The Primal Scream* (N.Y.: Dell Publishing Co., Inc. 1970) p. 25.
4. Ibid., p. 25.
5. Triton: *The Magic of Space*, pp. 138-149, cited by Jon Mundy: "On Fear," in: *Spiritual Frontiers*; Vol. IV (Summer, 1972), no. 3, p. 171.
6. Dr. William Kraft: *A Psychology of Nothingness* (Philadelphia: Westminister Press, 1974) p. 28.
7. Ibid., p. 104.
8. Dr. Carl Rogers: *On Becoming a Person* (Boston: Houghton Mifflin Company, 1961) p. 171.